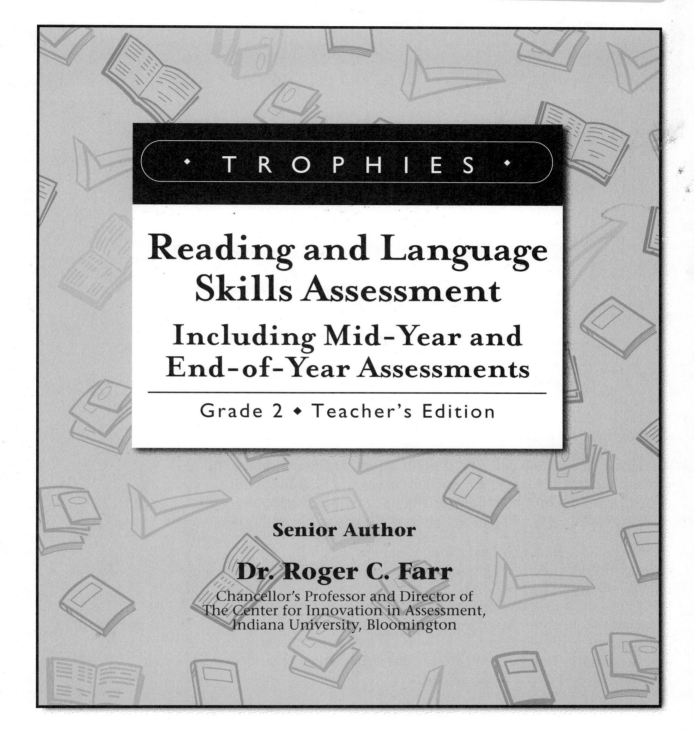

· TROPHIES ·

Reading and Language Skills Assessment

Including Mid-Year and End-of-Year Assessments

Grade 2 ◆ Teacher's Edition

Senior Author

Dr. Roger C. Farr

Chancellor's Professor and Director of
The Center for Innovation in Assessment,
Indiana University, Bloomington

Harcourt

Orlando   Boston   Dallas   Chicago   San Diego

Visit *The Learning Site!*

www.harcourtschool.com

Printed in the United States of America

ISBN 0-15-324962-5

6 7 8 9 10   170   10 09 08 07 06 05 04

Table of Contents

© Harcourt • Reading and Language Skills Assessment

Appendix

· ·

Trophies
Assessment Components

$\cdots\cdots\cdots\cdots\cdots\cdots\cdots\cdots\cdots\cdots\cdots\cdots\cdots\cdots\cdots$

The chart below gives a brief overview of the assessment choices that are available at this grade level. The titles in boldface can be found in this Teacher's Edition.

Entry-Level Assessments	**To plan instruction**
Placement and Diagnostic Assessments	◆ To determine the best placement for a student and to diagnose strengths and weaknesses
Reading and Language Skills Pretests	◆ To determine a student's proficiency with selected skills *before* starting instruction
Formative Assessments	**To monitor student progress**
End-of-Selection Tests	◆ To monitor a student's comprehension of each selection and selection vocabulary
Oral Reading Fluency Assessment	◆ To monitor the rate and accuracy with which a student reads text aloud
Assessment notes at "point of use" in the Teacher's Edition	◆ To monitor selected skills and strategies as they are taught
Mid-Year Reading and Language Skills Assessment	◆ To monitor how well a student has retained reading and language skills
Summative Assessments	**To assess mastery of skills taught** **To assess ability to apply skills and strategies**
Reading and Language Skills Posttests	◆ To assess mastery of reading and language skills taught in a theme
Holistic Assessment	◆ To evaluate a student's ability to apply reading and writing skills and strategies to new situations
End-of-Year Reading and Language Skills Assessment	◆ To evaluate mastery of reading and language skills taught during the year

Overview of the Teacher's Edition

This Teacher's Edition is organized into two major sections. Each section contains information about a separate assessment component. The two assessment components are as follows:

Reading and Language Skills Assessments

Two parallel forms of the *Reading and Language Skills Assessments*, a Pretest and a Posttest, are available for each theme at this grade. These assessments evaluate the specific skills taught in the themes. The assessments can be used in tandem before and after instruction in the theme, or they can be used independently. For example, only the posttest could be used to evaluate how well students learned the skills taught in the theme.

Mid-Year and End-of-Year Skills Assessments

Two cumulative assessments are also included in this Teacher's Edition. The *Mid-Year Reading and Language Skills Assessment* evaluates the skills taught in *Just for You*, Themes 1 through 3. The *End-of-Year Reading and Language Skills Assessment* evaluates the skills taught in *Just for You*, Themes 1 through 3, and *Banner Days*, Themes 1 through 3.

Copying masters for all of the assessment booklets are located in the Appendix. They are organized as follows:

Just for You/Theme 1   *Reading and Language Skills Assessment*
Just for You/Theme 2   *Reading and Language Skills Assessment*
Just for You/Theme 3   *Reading and Language Skills Assessment*
Mid-Year Reading and Language Skills Assessment

Banner Days/Theme 1   *Reading and Language Skills Assessment*
Banner Days/Theme 2   *Reading and Language Skills Assessment*
Banner Days/Theme 3   *Reading and Language Skills Assessment*
End-of-Year Reading and Language Skills Assessment

Reading and Language Skills Assessments

Description of the Assessments

The *Reading and Language Skills Assessments* are criterion-referenced tests designed to measure children's achievement on the skills taught in each of the themes. Criterion-referenced scores help teachers make decisions regarding the type of additional instruction that children may need.

Six *Reading and Language Skills Assessments* are available at this grade level—one assessment for each theme. The assessments evaluate children's achievement in decoding/phonics, vocabulary, literary response and analysis, comprehension, and language. The formats used on the *Reading and Language Skills Assessments* follow the same style as those used in instruction. This ensures that the assessments are aligned with the instruction.

Scheduling the Assessments

The *Reading and Language Skills Assessments* have been designed to correlate with specific skills introduced and reinforced within each theme of the program. Therefore, a *Reading and Language Skills Assessment Pretest* could be administered before a theme is started to determine which skills need to be emphasized. Or, a *Reading and Language Skills Assessment Posttest* could be administered after a theme is completed to verify that children can apply the skills that were taught.

If possible, a *Reading and Language Skills Assessment* should be given in one session. The pace at which you administer the assessment will depend on your particular class and group. The assessments are not timed. Most children should be able to complete an assessment in thirty to forty-five minutes.

Directions for Administering

The *Reading and Language Skills Assessments* are classroom assessments, not standardized tests. This means that teachers have some flexibility in how the assessments are administered. The following guidelines are intended to suggest, not prescribe, how to administer the assessments. Modify the directions to suit the needs of your children.

Prior to administering a *Reading and Language Skills Assessment*, you might read the following general directions to children.

Say: *Today you will be answering questions about some of the things we have learned together in class. Do your very best and try to answer each of the questions.*

Point out to children that the *Reading and Language Skills Assessment* is made up of different types of questions. Therefore, it is important to pay careful attention to the directions. For example, you might **say:**

It is very important to pay careful attention to the directions that I will read to you. The directions change during the test, so you must listen carefully as we work the sample questions.

Point out the "GO ON" and "STOP" signs at the bottom of each page. Explain that for each section of the assessment, the class will work a sample question together. Then children will read and answer questions on their own, following the "GO ON" signs. When they reach a "STOP" sign, they should stop and wait for the teacher to explain the next sample.

Say: *Open your booklets to page (_____). Now fold the other pages back so that only this page is facing up. Find the Sample question. Let's work the Sample question together.*

Hold up a demonstration copy for children to see. Check to be sure that every child is on the correct page. Then go through the Sample item with the class, making sure that every child understands what to do and how to mark the answers. Tell children to work until they come to the word "STOP." When they come to the word "STOP," they should put their pencils down and wait until the class is ready to begin the next subtest. When all children are ready to proceed to the next subtest, repeat the same procedure for the next subtest.

Although the procedures for administering each assessment are pretty straightforward, directions vary from category to category. The following table summarizes the specific directions for administering each skill category.

Skill Category	Subcategory	Directions
Decoding/Phonics	Vowels	• Read the model word(s) at the top of the sample. • Read the sentence that has a blank in it where a word is missing. • Choose the word that completes the sentence and also has the same sound as the underlined part of the model word(s).
	Abbreviations	Choose the correct abbreviation for each underlined word.
	Inflectional endings	Choose the correct form of the word to complete the sentence.
	Contractions	Choose the correct contraction for the underlined words.
	Prefixes and Suffixes	• Read the sentence with the blank. • Use the prefix or suffix to help choose the word that belongs in the sentence.
Vocabulary	Synonyms	Read the sentence with a blank. Choose the word that means the same thing as the underlined word in the sentence.
	Antonyms	Read the sentence with a blank. Choose the word that means the opposite of the underlined word in the sentence.
	Multiple-Meaning Words	Read each sentence. Use context clues to determine the meaning of the word each question asks about.
	Homophones	Read the four sentences. One sentence has the underlined homophone used incorrectly. Choose the sentence that is wrong.
Comprehension	Contents vary by theme.	Read the passage. Then read the questions that follow the passage, and choose the correct answer for each question.
	Interpret Information	Look at the chart or graph. Use the information on the chart or graph to help answer the questions that follow.
	Locate Information: Book Parts	Look at the sample glossary page, index, or table of contents page. Use these sample book parts to answer the questions that follow.
Literary Response and Analysis	Narrative Elements	Read the passage. Then read the questions that follow the passage, and choose the correct answer for each question.
Language	Contents vary by theme.	Read each question. Then choose the best answer for each question.

Harcourt • Reading and Language Skills Assessment

Since formats on a couple of the subtests (e.g., Decoding/Phonics and Vocabulary) may be unfamiliar to children, careful monitoring is advisable to make sure children understand what they are to do. Feel free to help children who have difficulty. For example, you might **say:**

If you have difficulty understanding any of the directions or questions, raise your hand and I will try to help you.

If necessary, make accommodations for children who have Individualized Education Plans that call for accommodations during testing, or for children who are just acquiring English. Record on the cover of the child's test booklet the type of accommodation made.

There are no time limits. Give children ample time to demonstrate what they know. Most children should complete the *Reading and Language Skills Assessment* in approximately 30 minutes.

Scoring and Interpreting the Assessments

The *Reading and Language Skills Assessment* can be scored using the answer keys. Follow these steps:

1. Turn to the appropriate answer key in the Appendix.
2. Compare the student's responses, item by item, to the answer key and put a check mark next to each item that is correctly answered.
3. Count the number of correct responses for each skill or subtest and write this number on the "Pupil Score" line on the booklet cover. Add the Pupil Scores for each skill to obtain the Total Score.
4. Determine if the child met the criterion for each skill.

A child who scores at or above the criterion level for each subtest is considered competent in that skill area and is probably ready to move forward without additional practice. A column for writing comments about "Pupil Strength" has been provided on the cover of the assessment booklet.

A child who does not reach criterion level probably needs additional instruction and/or practice in that particular skill. Examine the child's scores for each subtest and decide whether you should reteach a particular skill, or move forward to the next theme.

For teachers who wish to keep a cumulative record of Pupil Scores across themes, a Student Record Form has been provided for that purpose in the Appendix.

A *Reading and Language Skills Assessment* is just one observation of a child's reading behavior. It should be combined with other evidence of a child's progress, such as the teacher's daily observations, student work samples, and individual reading conferences. The sum of all of this information, coupled with test scores, is more reliable and valid than any single piece of information.

Mid-Year and End-of-Year Reading and Language Skills Assessments

Description of the Assessments

The *Mid-Year* and *End-of-Year Reading and Language Skills Assessments* are criterion-referenced tests designed to measure children's achievement on the skills taught in the themes. The assessments evaluate achievement in decoding/phonics, vocabulary, literary response and analysis, comprehension, and language. The assessments are designed to give a global picture of how well children apply the skills taught in the program. They are not intended to be diagnostic tests and do not yield specific scores for each skill. However, if a child does not reach the overall criterion for the total test, it is possible to judge his or her performance on the major skill categories (e.g., decoding/phonics, vocabulary, and comprehension).

The formats used on the *Mid-Year* and *End-of-Year Reading and Language Skills Assessments* follow the same style as those used in instruction. This ensures that the assessments are aligned with the instruction.

Contents of the Assessments

The following tables list the contents of the *Mid-Year* and *End-of-Year Assessments*. The contents of the *Mid-Year Reading and Language Skills Assessment* come from the skills taught in *Just for You*, Themes 1, 2, and 3. The contents of the *End-of-Year Reading and Language Skills Assessment* come from the skills taught in *Just for You*, Themes 1, 2, and 3, and *Banner Days*, Themes 1, 2, and 3.

Mid-Year Reading and Language Skills Assessment

Skill Category	Subcategory	Objective	Items
Decoding/Phonics	*R*-controlled Vowels	Decode words with *r*-controlled vowels (/ûr/*ear*, /ôr/*our*, /ir/*ear, eer*)	1–6, 10–12
Decoding/Phonics	Abbreviations	Decode words with common abbreviations	7–9
Decoding/Phonics	Vowel Digraphs	Decode words with vowel digraphs (/ $\overline{oo}$ /*oo*)	13–15
Decoding/Phonics	Inflectional Endings	Decode nouns and verbs with inflectional endings (*-s, -es, ies*; *y* to *i*)	16–18
Vocabulary	Synonyms	Recognize words that mean the same	19–22
Comprehension	Main Idea	Use text structure to identify the main idea in a passage	27, 29
Comprehension	Details	Identify supporting details in a passage	28, 30
Comprehension	Compare and Contrast	Recognize and analyze text presented in a compare/contrast format	23, 32
Comprehension	Sequence	Recognize and analyze text that is presented in sequential or chronological order	24, 31
Comprehension	Make Inferences	Use information from a reading selection and prior knowledge to make appropriate inferences	25–26
Comprehension	Interpret Information	Use charts, graphs, and diagrams to locate information	33–36
Comprehension	Follow Two-Step Written Directions	Understand and follow written instructions	37–40
Language		Display command of standard English conventions	41–50

End-of-Year Reading and Language Skills Assessment

Skill Category	Subcategory	Objective	Items
Decoding/Phonics	Vowel Diphthongs	Decode words with vowel diphthongs (/ou/*ou, ow*; /oi/*oi, oy*)	1–4
Decoding/Phonics	Vowel Digraphs	Decode words with vowel digraphs (/o͞o/*oo, ue, ew, ui, ou, ou[gh]*)	5–6
Decoding/Phonics	Inflectional Endings	Decode nouns and verbs with inflectional endings (*-es; f* to *v*)	7–8
Decoding/Phonics	Suffixes	Decode words with suffixes (*-ful, -less, -ing, -ly, -er, -est*)	9–10, 15–16
Decoding/Phonics	Contractions	Decode words with contractions (*'ll, n't, 's*)	11–12
Decoding/Phonics	Prefixes	Decode words with prefixes (*re-, pre-, mis-, under-, over-, un-*)	13–14
Decoding/Phonics	*R*-controlled Vowels	Decode words with *r*-controlled vowels (/âr/*air, are*)	17–18
Decoding/Phonics	Vowel Variants	Decode words with vowel variants (/o͝o/*oo, ou*; /ô/*aw, au[gh]*)	19–22
Vocabulary	Antonyms	Recognize words that mean the opposite	23–24
Vocabulary	Multiple-Meaning Words	Use context to determine meaning of multiple-meaning words	25–26
Vocabulary	Homophones	Use context to determine meaning of homophones	27–28
Comprehension	Main Idea	Use text structure to identify the main idea in a passage	29
Comprehension	Details	Identify supporting details in a passage	31
Comprehension	Cause and Effect	Analyze cause-and-effect relationships in text	30, 32
Comprehension	Summarize/Restate Information	Recognize a summary of a passage	33
Comprehension	Locate Information: Book Parts	Use book parts to locate information	34–36
Literary Response and Analysis	Narrative Elements	Identify plot, setting, and character in a story	37–40
Language		Display command of standard English conventions	41–50

Scheduling the Assessments

The *Mid-Year* and *End-of-Year Reading and Language Skills Assessments* have been designed to correlate with specific skills introduced and reinforced within each theme of the program. Each major reading skill taught in the program is represented on the assessments. The *Mid-Year* and *End-of-Year Reading Skills Assessments* are summative tests. That is, they are designed to evaluate whether children can apply the skills learned.

The *Mid-Year Reading and Language Skills Assessment* may be given after a child has completed the first three themes of instruction at this grade level. The *End-of-Year Reading and Language Skills Assessment* may be given after a child has completed all six themes of instruction at this grade level.

The *Mid-Year* and *End-of-Year Reading and Language Skills Assessments* should be given in one session, if possible. The pace at which you administer the assessments will depend on your particular class and group. The assessments are not timed. Most children should be able to complete each assessment in approximately forty-five minutes to an hour.

Directions for Administering

To administer the *Mid-Year* and *End-of-Year Reading and Language Skills Assessments*, follow the same procedures that you used to administer the *Reading and Language Skills Assessments* for each theme.

- Give a general introduction to the assessment and explain the purpose for using it.

- Guide students through the Sample item for the first section of the test. Make sure that all students understand what they are to do.

- Encourage students to work independently, following the "GO ON" signs and stopping when they reach a "STOP" sign.

- Repeat this process for each section of the assessment.

Remember, you may modify the directions to suit the needs of your children.

Teacher's Edition

Scoring and Interpreting the Assessments

The *Mid-Year and End-of-Year Reading Skills Assessments* can be scored by using the answer keys found in the Appendix. Follow these steps:

1. Turn to the appropriate answer key in the Appendix.

2. Compare the student's responses, item by item, to the answer key, and put a check mark next to each item that is correctly answered.

3. Count the number of correct responses for each skill category and write that number on the "Pupil Score" line on the cover of the assessment booklet. Add the Pupil Scores for each skill category to obtain the student's Total Score.

4. Next, determine if the child met the criterion for Total Score. The criterion score can be found on the cover page of the assessment booklet. Use the "Interpreting Performance" chart found in this section of the Teacher's Edition booklet to interpret the student's score.

5. If a child does not reach the overall criterion on the total test, you may evaluate the child's performance on particular skill categories. Look at each skill category and determine if the child met the criterion for that skill category. Then determine the child's strengths and weaknesses for particular skill categories. Write comments in the space provided.

There are 50 items on the *Mid-Year Reading and Language Skills Assessment* and 50 items on the *End-of-Year Reading and Language Skills Assessment*. For each item, a correct answer should be given 1 point, and an incorrect or missing answer should be given 0 points. Thus, a perfect score on each of the assessments would be 50. Use the following performance chart to interpret score ranges.

Interpreting Performance on the
Mid-Year and *End-of-Year Reading Skills Assessments*

Total Score	Interpretation	Teaching Suggestions
Mid-Year: 36–50 **End-of-Year: 36–50**	Average to excellent understanding and use of the major reading and language skills	Children scoring at the high end of this range exceed the criterion and should have no difficulty moving forward to the next level of the program. Children scoring at the low end of this range meet the criterion and are performing at an acceptable level.
Mid-Year: 0–35 **End-of-Year: 0–35**	Fair to limited understanding and use of the major reading and language skills	Children scoring at the high end of this range are performing slightly below the criterion and may need extra help before or after moving to the next level of the program. Note whether performance varied across the skill categories tested. Examine other samples of the students' work and/or administer some of the individual assessments (e.g., Phonics Inventory, Oral Reading Fluency Assessment) to confirm their progress and pinpoint instructional needs. Children scoring at the low end of this range do not meet criterion and should have their performance verified through other measures such as some of the individual assessments available in this program, or daily work samples. Identify what specific instructional needs must be met by reviewing the student's performance on each skill category.

A child who does not reach the criterion level may not do so for a variety of reasons. Use the questions that follow to better understand why a child may not have reached the criterion.

• *Has the child completed all parts of the program being tested on the assessment?*

If not, the results may not be valid, since the *Mid-Year Reading and Language Skills Assessment* evaluates all the major skills taught in the first three themes at this grade level, and the *End-of-Year Reading and Language Skills Assessment* evaluates the major skills taught in all six themes at this grade level. It would be unfair to expect a child to demonstrate mastery of skills for which he or she has not received instruction.

• *Was the child having a bad day when he or she took the assessment?*

Children can experience social or emotional problems that may affect concentration and influence performance. Sometimes a problem at home or a conflict on the school playground carries over into the classroom and interferes with performance. Recall any unusual behavior you observed before or during the testing, or confer with the child to identify any factors that may have adversely affected performance. If the child's limited performance can be attributed to extraneous problems, readminister the assessment under better conditions or discard the results.

• *Does the child perform differently on group tests than on individual tests?*

Student performance can fluctuate depending on the context and mode of the assessment. Some children perform better in a one-on-one setting that fosters individual attention than they do in a group setting that is less personal. Others are more successful reading orally than reading silently. Likewise, some children feel more comfortable answering open-ended questions orally than they do answering multiple-choice questions on a paper-and-pencil test.

• *Does the child perform differently on tests than on daily activities?*

Compare the child's performance on the mid-year and the end-of-year assessment with his or her performance on other formal types of assessment, such as theme tests and standardized tests. Also note how the child's performance compares with his or her performance on informal types of assessment, such as portfolios, reading logs, and anecdotal observation records. If the results are similar, it would suggest that the mid-year and the end-of-year results are valid and accurately represent the child's performance. If the results are not consistent, explore alternative explanations.

To resolve conflicts regarding the child's performance, you may want to collect additional evidence. For example, you may want to administer some of the individual assessments available with this program (e.g., Phonics Inventory, Oral Reading Fluency Assessment).

As with all assessments, it is important not to place too much faith in a single test. The *Mid-Year* and *End-of-Year Reading and Language Skills Assessments* are just one observation of a child's reading behavior. They should be combined with other evidence of a child's progress, such as the teacher's daily observations, the child's work samples, and individual reading conferences. The sum of all this information, combined with test scores, is more reliable and valid than any single piece of information.

Appendix

• •

Answer Keys for *Reading and Language Skills Assessments: Pretests and Posttests*

Just for You/Theme 1

PRETEST	POSTTEST
COMPREHENSION: **Main Idea**	**COMPREHENSION:** **Main Idea**
1. A	1. B
2. D	2. A
3. B	3. D
4. A	4. C
COMPREHENSION: **Compare/Contrast**	**COMPREHENSION:** **Compare/Contrast**
5. C	5. A
6. B	6. C
7. D	7. D
8. D	8. C
9. C	9. D
10. A	10. A
11. B	11. A
12. D	12. C
LANGUAGE	**LANGUAGE**
13. B	13. C
14. A	14. B
15. C	15. A
16. B	16. C
17. C	17. B
18. A	18. C
19. B	19. B
20. C	20. A
21. B	21. A
22. A	22. B

Answer Keys for *Reading and Language Skills Assessments: Pretests and Posttests*

Just for You/Theme 2

PRETEST	POSTTEST
DECODING/PHONICS	**DECODING/PHONICS**
1. B	1. C
2. A	2. B
3. C	3. D
4. D	4. A
5. C	5. B
6. B	6. D
7. A	7. A
8. B	8. C
9. C	9. B
10. B	10. C
11. A	11. D
12. D	12. A
VOCABULARY:	**VOCABULARY:**
Synonyms	**Synonyms**
13. B	13. A
14. A	14. B
15. B	15. D
16. C	16. C
COMPREHENSION:	**COMPREHENSION:**
Sequence	**Sequence**
17. B	17. C
18. C	18. D
19. A	19. A
20. C	20. C
LANGUAGE	**LANGUAGE**
21. A	21. B
22. B	22. A
23. A	23. A
24. B	24. B
25. A	25. C
26. A	26. A
27. C	27. B
28. B	28. A
29. A	29. C
30. A	30. B

Answer Keys for *Reading and Language Skills Assessments:*
Pretests and Posttests
Just for You/Theme 3

PRETEST	POSTTEST
DECODING/PHONICS	**DECODING/PHONICS**

PRETEST

DECODING/PHONICS

1. C	7. D
2. A	8. C
3. A	9. B
4. D	10. A
5. B	11. D
6. A	12. B

COMPREHENSION:
Interpret Information
13. B
14. A
15. C
16. B

COMPREHENSION:
Details
17. C
18. B
19. D
20. A

COMPREHENSION:
Make Inferences
21. B
22. B
23. A
24. D

COMPREHENSION:
Follow Two-Step Written
Directions
25. C
26. B
27. A
28. C

LANGUAGE
29. B
30. C
31. A
32. B
33. C
34. B
35. A
36. B
37. A
38. C

POSTTEST

DECODING/PHONICS

1. B	7. C
2. A	8. D
3. B	9. C
4. C	10. A
5. B	11. D
6. A	12. B

COMPREHENSION:
Interpret Information
13. B
14. B
15. A
16. D

COMPREHENSION:
Details
17. C
18. B
19. D
20. C

COMPREHENSION:
Make Inferences
21. C
22. A
23. B
24. C

COMPREHENSION:
Follow Two-Step Written
Directions
25. C
26. A
27. D
28. B

LANGUAGE
29. A
30. B
31. A
32. C
33. B
34. C
35. B
36. A
37. B
38. B

Answer Keys for *Reading and Language Skills Assessments: Pretests and Posttests*
Banner Days/Theme 1

PRETEST	POSTTEST
DECODING/PHONICS	**DECODING/PHONICS**
1. C	1. C
2. B	2. B
3. A	3. A
4. B	4. A
5. B	5. C
6. A	6. B
7. B	7. D
8. C	8. A
9. C	9. D
10. A	10. B
11. D	11. A
12. B	12. C
13. B	13. C
14. D	14. A
15. A	15. D
16. C	16. B
17. C	17. C
18. B	18. D
19. A	19. A
20. D	20. B
VOCABULARY:	**VOCABULARY:**
Antonyms	**Antonyms**
21. B	21. D
22. C	22. C
23. D	23. B
24. A	24. A
COMPREHENSION:	**COMPREHENSION:**
Cause and Effect	**Cause and Effect**
25. A	25. B
26. C	26. C
27. B	27. B
28. D	28. D
LANGUAGE	**LANGUAGE**
29. B	29. B
30. C	30. A
31. A	31. C
32. C	32. C
33. B	33. B
34. B	34. A
35. A	35. B
36. B	36. C
37. C	37. B
38. B	38. C

Answer Keys for *Reading and Language Skills Assessments:*
Pretests and Posttests
*Banner Days/*Theme 2

PRETEST	POSTTEST
DECODING/PHONICS	**DECODING/PHONICS**

PRETEST

DECODING/PHONICS

1. D	9. A
2. A	10. B
3. B	11. A
4. C	12. C
5. D	13. B
6. B	14. C
7. C	15. C
8. A	16. B

VOCABULARY:
Multiple-Meaning Words
17. A
18. C
19. B
20. A

COMPREHENSION:
Summarize/Restate
Information
21. C
22. D
23. B
24. B

LITERARY RESPONSE AND
ANALYSIS:
Narrative Elements
25. B
26. C
27. B
28. A

LANGUAGE
29. B
30. C
31. A
32. B
33. C
34. B
35. C
36. A
37. B
38. C

POSTTEST

DECODING/PHONICS

1. A	9. B
2. B	10. D
3. D	11. A
4. B	12. C
5. C	13. B
6. B	14. C
7. A	15. B
8. C	16. C

VOCABULARY:
Multiple-Meaning Words
17. B
18. C
19. C
20. A

COMPREHENSION:
Summarize/Restate
Information
21. B
22. B
23. C
24. A

LITERARY RESPONSE AND
ANALYSIS:
Narrative Elements
25. C
26. D
27. C
28. B

LANGUAGE
29. B
30. B
31. A
32. B
33. C
34. B
35. C
36. A
37. A
38. C

Teacher's Edition

Answer Keys for *Reading and Language Skills Assessments:*
Pretests and Posttests
Banner Days/Theme 3

PRETEST		POSTTEST	
DECODING/PHONICS		**DECODING/PHONICS**	
1. B	11. D	1. B	11. D
2. C	12. A	2. C	12. C
3. B	13 B	3. B	13 A
4. A	14. A	4. A	14. A
5. B	15. C	5. C	15. D
6. C	16. B	6. A	16. B
7. A	17. C	7. B	17. C
8. B	18. B	8. B	18. B
9. A	19. A	9. C	19. A
10. B	20. B	10. A	20. D
VOCABULARY:		**VOCABULARY:**	
Homophones		**Homophones**	
21. B		21. C	
22. C		22. A	
23. D		23. B	
24. A		24. D	
COMPREHENSION:		**COMPREHENSION:**	
Locate Information		**Locate Information**	
25. A		25. B	
26. C		26. B	
27. B		27. C	
28. C		28. A	
29. C		29. D	
30. B		30. A	
LANGUAGE		**LANGUAGE**	
31. A		31. B	
32. B		32. C	
33. B		33. B	
34. C		34. A	
35. B		35. B	
36. A		36. A	
37. A		37. A	
38. B		38. B	
39. C		39. C	
40. B		40. B	

Answer Key
Mid-Year Reading and Language Skills Assessment

DECODING/PHONICS

1. B
2. D
3. A
4. C
5. D
6. A
7. B
8. B
9. C
10. B
11. A
12. C
13. C
14. B
15. D
16. B
17. A
18. D

VOCABULARY

19. B
20. A
21. B
22. C

COMPREHENSION

23. B
24. C

25. C
26. A
27. D
28. A
29. C
30. D
31. B
32. A
33. D
34. C
35. A
36. B
37. C
38. D
39. C
40. A

LANGUAGE

41. B
42. A
43. C
44. B
45. A
46. C
47. A
48. B
49. C
50. A

Teacher's Edition

Answer Key
End-of-Year Reading and Language Skills Assessment

DECODING/PHONICS
1. B
2. C
3. A
4. C
5. A
6. B
7. B
8. C
9. C
10. B
11. D
12. B
13. B
14. A
15. B
16. C
17. A
18. D
19. C
20. B
21. A
22. D

VOCABULARY
23. B
24. A
25. A
26. D
27. B
28. C

COMPREHENSION
29. B
30. B
31. D
32. C
33. B
34. D
35. B
36. C

LITERARY RESPONSE AND ANALYSIS
37. B
38. C
39. D
40. D

LANGUAGE
41. C
42. B
43. B
44. C
45. B
46. A
47. B
48. A
49. C
50. B

Student Record Form
Reading and Language Skills Assessment
Trophies
Grade 2

Name _____ **Grade** _____

Teacher _____

	CRITERION SCORE	PUPIL SCORE	COMMENTS
Just for You/Theme 1			
Main Idea	3/4	___/4	_____
Compare and Contrast	6/8	___/8	_____
Language	7/10	___/10	_____
Just for You/Theme 2			
R-controlled Vowels (/ûr/*ear*)	3/4	___/4	_____
R-controlled Vowels (/ôr/*our*)	3/4	___/4	_____
Abbreviations	3/4	___/4	_____
Synonyms	3/4	___/4	_____
Sequence	3/4	___/4	_____
Language	7/10	___/10	_____
Just for You/Theme 3			
R-controlled Vowels (/ir/*ear, eer*)	3/4	___/4	_____
Vowel Digraphs($\overline{oo}$/*oo*)	3/4	___/4	_____
Inflectional Endings(-*s, -es, -ies*)	3/4	___/4	_____
Interpret Information: Charts, Graphs, Diagrams	3/4	___/4	_____
Details	3/4	___/4	_____
Make Inferences	3/4	___/4	_____
Follow Two-Step Written Directions	3/4	___/4	_____
Language	7/10	___/10	_____

Student Record Form
Reading and Language Skills Assessment
Trophies
Grade 2

Name _____ Grade _____

Teacher _____

	CRITERION SCORE	PUPIL SCORE	COMMENTS
Banner Days/Theme 1			
Vowel Diphthongs (/ou/*ou, ow*)	3/4	___/4	_____
Vowel Diphthongs (/oi/*oi, oy*)	3/4	___/4	_____
Vowel Digraphs (o͞o/*oo, ue*)	3/4	___/4	_____
Inflectional Endings (*-es*)	3/4	___/4	_____
Suffixes (*-ing, -ly, -ful, -less*)	3/4	___/4	_____
Antonyms	3/4	___/4	_____
Cause and Effect	3/4	___/4	_____
Language	7/10	___/10	_____
Banner Days/Theme 2			
Vowel Digraphs (/o͞o/*ew, ui*)	3/4	___/4	_____
Contractions (*'ll, n't, 's*)	3/4	___/4	_____
Prefixes (*re-, pre-, mis-, under-*)	3/4	___/4	_____
Suffixes (*-er, -est*)	3/4	___/4	_____
Multiple-Meaning Words	3/4	___/4	_____
Summarize/Restate Information	3/4	___/4	_____
Narrative Elements	3/4	___/4	_____
Language	7/10	___/10	_____
Banner Days/Theme 3			
R-controlled Vowels (/âr/*air, are*)	3/4	___/4	_____
Vowel Variants (/o͝o/*oo, ou*)	3/4	___/4	_____
Vowel Variants (/ô/*aw, au[gh]*)	3/4	___/4	_____
Vowel Digraphs (/o͞o/*ou, ou[gh]*)	3/4	___/4	_____
Prefixes (*over-, un-*)	3/4	___/4	_____
Homophones	3/4	___/4	_____
Locate Information: Book Parts	4/6	___/6	_____
Language	7/10	___/10	_____

· T R O P H I E S ·

Reading and Language Skills
Assessment Pretest

Just for You / Theme 1

Name _____ Date _____

SKILL AREA	Criterion Score	Pupil Score	Pupil Strength
COMPREHENSION			
Main Idea	3/4	_____	_____
Compare/Contrast	6/8	_____	_____
LANGUAGE Sentences Statements and Questions Commands and Exclamations Naming Parts of Sentences Telling Parts of Sentences	7/10	_____	_____
TOTAL SCORE	16/22	_____	_____

Were accommodations made in administering this test? ☐ Yes ☐ No

Type of accommodations: _____

_____

COMPREHENSION: Main Idea

Having fun outdoors helps keep you well and strong. Some people like to swim or to fish. Many people like to run or to take walks. Other people like to play ball or other games. Getting out in the fresh air is good for you!

Sample

What is this story mostly about?

Ⓐ Some people like to swim or to fish.

Ⓑ Other people like to play ball or other games.

Ⓒ Having fun outdoors helps keep you well and strong.

Ⓓ Many people like to run or to take walks.

GO ON

COMPREHENSION: Main Idea (continued)

There are many things you should know to take good care of a cat. Cats need to be clean and dry and warm. If they sleep where it is cold, they might get sick.

Cats do not like to get wet, but they keep very clean anyway. A cat washes its face and paws every day.

Cats eat many different kinds of food. They like to eat meat and fish. Most cats like to drink milk or water.

1. What is this story mostly about?

Ⓐ There are many things you should know to take care of a cat.

Ⓑ If cats sleep where it is cold, they might get sick.

Ⓒ Cats do not like to get wet, but they keep very clean anyway.

Ⓓ Cats like to eat meat and fish.

GO ON

Harcourt • Reading and Language Skills Assessment

COMPREHENSION: Main Idea (continued)

> There are many different sizes and kinds of sharks. Some sharks are only 5 feet long. Other sharks may grow to be 40 or 50 feet long. The largest shark, the whale shark, eats only small sea animals and plants. The white shark, though, is a man-eater.

2. What is this story mostly about?

Ⓐ Some sharks are only 5 feet long.

Ⓑ The white shark is a man-eater.

Ⓒ The largest shark eats only small sea animals and plants.

Ⓓ There are many different sizes and kinds of sharks.

GO ON

COMPREHENSION: Main Idea (continued)

Long ago, before we had printed books, it took weeks or even months to write a book. For thousands of years, all books had to be written by hand. People had to use a brush, a reed, or a quill to write them with. No two books ever looked just alike. Not many people knew how to read then. As time went by, though, more and more people learned to read, and they wanted more books. In time, people learned how to print books instead of copying them by hand.

3. What is this story mostly about?

Ⓐ No two books ever looked just alike.

Ⓑ Before we had printed books, it took weeks or months to write a book by hand.

Ⓒ People had to use a brush, a reed, or a quill to write books with.

Ⓓ Not many people knew how to read then.

GO ON

Just for You / Theme 1

Harcourt • Reading and Language Skills Assessment

COMPREHENSION: Main Idea (continued)

Tony knows that reading is important. In the morning before school, he reads all the words on the cereal box. Sometimes he forgets the time, and he has to hurry to finish his breakfast.

On the school bus, Tony reads every sign he can see out the window. He learns many new words this way. One day he saw a sign for the zoo. He saw a picture of a big, gray animal. He learned to read the word *elephant*.

When Tony goes to bed at night, he always reads a story. Then, while he is asleep, he dreams of words.

4. What is this story mostly about?

Ⓐ Tony knows that reading is important.

Ⓑ Tony reads all the words on the cereal box.

Ⓒ Tony forgets the time sometimes and has to hurry.

Ⓓ Tony reads every sign he can see out the window.

STOP

COMPREHENSION: Compare and Contrast

Jim likes to play outside. He spends most of his time playing baseball or soccer with his friends. Jeff likes to stay inside and play video games with his friends. Both boys are nice and have many friends.

Sample

How are Jim and Jeff **alike**?

Ⓐ They like to play outside.

Ⓑ They have many friends.

Ⓒ They like to play video games.

Ⓓ They spend time playing soccer.

GO ON

COMPREHENSION: Compare and Contrast (continued)

Maylee and Jan are best friends. They both love pizza. They like pepperoni with extra cheese the most. Sometimes their mothers buy frozen pizza at the store to cook at home. At special times, the friends like to go out to eat together. They like pizza from different pizza parlors. Maylee likes pizza from Roman Pizza Parlor. She likes the kind with spicy sauce and thin, crispy crust. Jan likes to get pizza at Little Italy Pizza Parlor. She likes the deep-dish style with spicy sauce and thick, chewy crust. To make sure each gets the kind she likes, they take turns going to their favorite pizza parlors.

5. How are Maylee and Jan **alike**?
  Ⓐ They help their mothers shop at the store.
  Ⓑ They are learning to make pizza.
  Ⓒ They like pepperoni pizza.
  Ⓓ They are from Italy.

6. One way that Maylee is **different** from Jan is that Maylee likes _____.
  Ⓐ extra cheese
  Ⓑ thin, crispy crust
  Ⓒ thick, chewy crust
  Ⓓ spicy sauce

GO ON

COMPREHENSION: Compare and Contrast (continued)

7. At special times, **both** friends like to _____.

    Ⓐ get pizza at the store

    Ⓑ try different kinds of pizza

    Ⓒ cook pizza at home

    Ⓓ go out to eat pizza

8. When the friends go out to eat, they choose **different** _____.

    Ⓐ sauces

    Ⓑ toppings

    Ⓒ cheese

    Ⓓ pizza parlors

GO ON ▶

COMPREHENSION: Compare and Contrast (continued)

> The Clarks have two dogs. The dogs are friendly and playful, and they obey commands. Rusty is a small cocker spaniel with wavy golden hair. He has long, soft ears and a stubby tail. He loves to take long walks in the woods with Mrs. Clark. Rusty is a quiet dog, so he stays in the house most of the time. Levi is a big golden lab with bright brown eyes. He is very jumpy, and his long tail is very strong. When he wags it, he sometimes knocks things over. He barks loudly, so he stays in the backyard most of the time. Levi likes to ride in the truck with Mr. Clark.

9. How are Rusty and Levi **alike**?

Ⓐ They like to take long walks.

Ⓑ They stay in the backyard.

Ⓒ They are friendly and playful.

Ⓓ They have stubby tails.

10. One way Levi is **different** from Rusty is that Levi likes to _____.

Ⓐ ride in the truck

Ⓑ walk in the woods

Ⓒ stay in the house

Ⓓ be very quiet

GO ON

COMPREHENSION: Compare and Contrast (continued)

11. When the Clarks give commands, **both** dogs _____.

Ⓐ play

Ⓑ obey

Ⓒ jump

Ⓓ bark

12. Rusty is small, and Levi is big, but **both** dogs have _____.

Ⓐ soft ears

Ⓑ long tails

Ⓒ loud barks

Ⓓ golden hair

STOP

Harcourt • Reading and Language Skills Assessment

LANGUAGE

Sample

Which group of words is a correct sentence?

(A) Ran to greet me.

(B) Her pets and mine.

(C) I have three fish.

---

13. Which group of words is a correct sentence?

(A) Reads about ants.

(B) Jim likes ice cream.

(C) My friend Ann.

14. Which group of words is a correct sentence?

(A) I played three games.

(B) I games three played.

(C) I three played games.

GO ON

LANGUAGE (continued)

15. Which sentence is a statement?

Ⓐ Did you hear that sound?

Ⓑ Will you go with me?

Ⓒ I put pickles on my sandwich.

16. Which sentence is a question?

Ⓐ Seth has a pet hamster.

Ⓑ May I see your picture?

Ⓒ Sara can run fast.

17. Which statement begins and ends correctly?

Ⓐ he can sing well

Ⓑ he can sing well.

Ⓒ He can sing well.

18. Which sentence is an exclamation?

Ⓐ What a big dog that is!

Ⓑ Open the window.

Ⓒ Please be quiet.

GO ON

LANGUAGE (continued)

19. Which sentence is a command?

Ⓐ How tall you have grown!

Ⓑ Do not walk on the grass.

Ⓒ What a good time we had!

20. What kind of sentence is this?

She likes baseball and soccer.

Ⓐ command

Ⓑ question

Ⓒ statement

21. Which answer tells about the underlined words?

The kite <u>sails high in the sky</u>.

Ⓐ naming part

Ⓑ telling part

Ⓒ complete sentence

22. Which answer tells about the underlined words?

<u>The sun</u> is bright today.

Ⓐ naming part

Ⓑ telling part

Ⓒ complete sentence

STOP

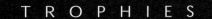

Being Me / Theme 1

Reading and Language Skills Assessment

Harcourt

Orlando   Boston   Dallas   Chicago   San Diego

Part No. 9997-37712-5

ISBN 0-15-332175-X (Package of 12)

2-1

Reading and Language Skills Assessment Posttest

Just for You / Theme 1

Name_____ Date_____

SKILL AREA	Criterion Score	Pupil Score	Pupil Strength
COMPREHENSION			
Main Idea	3/4	_____	_____
Compare/Contrast	6/8	_____	_____
LANGUAGE	7/10	_____	_____
Sentences			
Statements and Questions			
Commands and Exclamations			
Naming Parts of Sentences			
Telling Parts of Sentences			
TOTAL SCORE	16/22	_____	_____

Were accommodations made in administering this test? ❑ Yes ❑ No

Type of accommodations: _____

_____

ISBN 0-15-332175-X

6 7 8 9 10   170   10 09 08 07 06 05 04

COMPREHENSION: Main Idea

Having fun outdoors helps keep you well and strong. Some people like to swim or to fish. Many people like to run or to take walks. Other people like to play ball or other games. Getting out in the fresh air is good for you!

Sample

What is this story mostly about?

Ⓐ Some people like to swim or to fish.

Ⓑ Other people like to play ball or other games.

Ⓒ Having fun outdoors helps keep you well and strong.

Ⓓ Many people like to run or to take walks.

GO ON

COMPREHENSION: Main Idea (continued)

When our country was young, people lived differently from how we live today. People had to cut trees to build their own houses. They had to grow their own food. They also had to hunt or fish to get meat to eat. They had to cook their food over an open fire. They also had to chop their own firewood to keep them warm during the winter.

1. What is this story mostly about?

Ⓐ People had to cook their food over an open fire.

Ⓑ When our country was young, people lived differently from how we live today.

Ⓒ People had to grow their own food.

Ⓓ People had to hunt or fish to get meat to eat.

GO ON

Just for You / Theme 1

Harcourt • Reading and Language Skills Assessment

COMPREHENSION: Main Idea (continued)

The Big Dipper is an important picture in the night sky. It is made up of seven stars. To some people, the Big Dipper looks like a giant cup with a long handle. This picture is also known as the Big Bear. Some people think the seven stars look like a bear's body.

The Big Dipper is important. If you look up and out from the end of the cup you will see the North Star. If you get lost at night, you can figure out the right way to go.

2. What is this story mostly about?

Ⓐ The Big Dipper is an important picture in the night sky.

Ⓑ The Big Dipper is made up of seven stars.

Ⓒ Some people think the stars look like a bear's body.

Ⓓ To some people, the Big Dipper looks like a giant cup.

GO ON

COMPREHENSION: Main Idea (continued)

Living in a group is helpful to lions. A group of lions is called a *pride.* Some prides may have as many as 40 lions. Lions in a pride can protect each other from other animals. They can help each other take care of the baby lions. They can hunt together. They can watch over each other when they are resting.

3. What is this story mostly about?

Ⓐ Some prides may have as many as 40 lions.

Ⓑ Lions can protect each other from other animals.

Ⓒ Lions can watch over each other when they are resting.

Ⓓ Living in a group is helpful to lions.

GO ON

Harcourt • Reading and Language Skills Assessment

COMPREHENSION: Main Idea (continued)

Mrs. Garza works hard to grow a beautiful garden. All year long she works in her yard. Spring is the busiest time. Mrs. Garza digs in the earth to plant flowers and vegetables.

In the summer, Mrs. Garza stays busy. She pulls the weeds. She waters the young plants. When the vegetables are ready, she picks them.

In the fall, Mrs. Garza picks the last flowers and vegetables. She adds special food to the soil.

In the winter, the garden rests, but not Mrs. Garza. She plans her garden for next year. When spring comes, she will be ready.

4. What is this story mostly about?

Ⓐ In the summer, Mrs. Garza stays busy.

Ⓑ When the vegetables are ready, Mrs. Garza picks them.

Ⓒ Mrs. Garza works hard to grow a beautiful garden.

Ⓓ When spring comes, Mrs. Garza will be ready.

STOP

COMPREHENSION: Compare and Contrast

Jim likes to play outside. He spends most of his time playing baseball or soccer with his friends. Jeff likes to stay inside and play video games with his friends. Both boys are nice and have many friends.

Sample

How are Jim and Jeff **alike**?

Ⓐ They like to play outside.

Ⓑ They have many friends.

Ⓒ They like to play video games.

Ⓓ They spend time playing soccer.

GO ON

Harcourt • Reading and Language Skills Assessment

COMPREHENSION: Compare and Contrast (continued)

Aunt Maggie has a cabin in the country. She stays there for one week in the winter and three weeks in the summer. She thinks it is beautiful at both times of the year. In winter, soft white snow covers the ground. Aunt Maggie feeds the deer and rabbits that live nearby. She sometimes sees an eagle, but there are not very many birds. It is quiet and peaceful.

In the summer the country is warm and green. On hot afternoons, Aunt Maggie swims in the river. She watches all the birds that twitter noisily in the trees. She hears the chugging sound of tractors in the fields. She hears other swimmers enjoying the river.

5. How is Aunt Maggie's cabin **alike** in winter and summer?

Ⓐ Animals live nearby.

Ⓑ It is quiet and peaceful.

Ⓒ Tractors work in the fields.

Ⓓ There is snow on the ground.

GO ON

COMPREHENSION: Compare and Contrast (continued)

6. One way that winter at the cabin is **different** from summer is that in winter Aunt Maggie likes to _____.

Ⓐ ride the tractors

Ⓑ swim in the river

Ⓒ look for eagles

Ⓓ hear other swimmers

7. At **both** times of the year, Aunt Maggie thinks that the country is _____.

Ⓐ cold

Ⓑ noisy

Ⓒ crowded

Ⓓ beautiful

8. One way that the cabin is **different** in winter and summer is that in summer there are more _____.

Ⓐ fish

Ⓑ deer

Ⓒ birds

Ⓓ rabbits

GO ON

Harcourt • Reading and Language Skills Assessment

COMPREHENSION: Compare and Contrast (continued)

> The Martins have two cats. They are friendly and loving pets. They both come running when Mrs. Martin calls them by name. Belle is an old Persian cat with long gray fur and a full, bushy tail. She has a snubbed nose and small ears. Her legs are short and strong. Belle likes to rest quietly in Mrs. Martin's lap. Belle stays in the house most of the time, taking it easy or sleeping. Wilbur is a frisky young Manx cat. He has short golden fur and no tail. His strong rear legs are longer than his front legs. When he runs, he looks like a hopping rabbit. Wilbur likes to stay outside, climbing trees or chasing birds. Mr. Martin has even taught Wilbur to do some tricks.

9. How are Belle and Wilbur **alike**?

(A) They like to chase birds.

(B) They like to be outside.

(C) They have full, bushy tails.

(D) They are friendly and loving.

GO ON

COMPREHENSION: Compare and Contrast (continued)

10. One way Wilbur is **different** from Belle is that Wilbur likes to _____.

Ⓐ climb trees

Ⓑ take it easy

Ⓒ stay in the house

Ⓓ rest in Mrs. Martin's lap

11. When Mrs. Martin calls them by name, **both** cats _____.

Ⓐ come running

Ⓑ hop like rabbits

Ⓒ do tricks

Ⓓ meow

12. Belle is old, and Wilbur is young, but **both** cats have _____.

Ⓐ golden fur

Ⓑ bushy tails

Ⓒ strong legs

Ⓓ snubbed noses

STOP

Harcourt • Reading and Language Skills Assessment

LANGUAGE

Sample

Which group of words is a correct sentence?

Ⓐ Ran to greet me.

Ⓑ Her pets and mine.

Ⓒ I have three fish.

---

13. Which group of words is a correct sentence?

Ⓐ Learns about bees.

Ⓑ Some mice.

Ⓒ I love apple pie.

14. Which group of words is a correct sentence?

Ⓐ He pets four has.

Ⓑ He has four pets.

Ⓒ He four has pets.

GO ON

LANGUAGE (continued)

15. Which sentence is a statement?

Ⓐ The bell is ringing.

Ⓑ Would you like a cookie?

Ⓒ What color do you like?

16. Which sentence is a question?

Ⓐ I go to Benson School.

Ⓑ Here are some keys.

Ⓒ Who won the race?

17. Which statement begins and ends correctly?

Ⓐ my sister is two years old

Ⓑ My sister is two years old.

Ⓒ my sister is two years old.

18. Which sentence is an exclamation?

Ⓐ Please help me pack.

Ⓑ Do not be late.

Ⓒ How pretty the roses are!

GO ON

Harcourt • Reading and Language Skills Assessment

LANGUAGE (continued)

19. Which sentence is a command?

Ⓐ What a great show that was!

Ⓑ Print your name at the top.

Ⓒ How cold it is in here!

20. What kind of sentence is this?

Get in line now.

Ⓐ command

Ⓑ question

Ⓒ statement

21. Which answer tells about the underlined words?

<u>The kitten</u> played with the string.

Ⓐ naming part

Ⓑ telling part

Ⓒ complete sentence

22. Which answer tells about the underlined words?

The leaves <u>changed color</u>.

Ⓐ naming part

Ⓑ telling part

Ⓒ complete sentence

STOP

· T R O P H I E S ·

Being Me / Theme 1
Reading and Language Skills Assessment

Harcourt

Orlando   Boston   Dallas   Chicago   San Diego

Part No. 9997-37709-5

ISBN 0-15-332175-X (Package of 12)

2-1

TROPHIES

Reading and Language Skills
Assessment Pretest

Just for You / Theme 2

Name _____ Date _____

SKILL AREA	Criterion Score	Pupil Score	Pupil Strength
DECODING/PHONICS			
R-controlled Vowels			
/ûr/*ear*	3/4	_____	_____
/ôr/*our*	3/4	_____	_____
Abbreviations	3/4	_____	_____
VOCABULARY			
Synonyms	3/4	_____	_____
COMPREHENSION			
Sequence	3/4	_____	_____
LANGUAGE	7/10	_____	_____
Nouns			
Plural Nouns			
Names of People			
Animals and Places			
TOTAL SCORE	22/30	_____	_____

Were accommodations made in administering this test? ❑ Yes ❑ No

Type of accommodations: _____

_____

Printed in the United States of America

ISBN 0-15-332175-X

6 7 8 9 10   170   10 09 08 07 06 05 04

DECODING/PHONICS

<u>**earth**</u>

Sample

We will _____ songs in music class.

year	rehearse	sing	radish
Ⓐ	Ⓑ	Ⓒ	Ⓓ

1. We _____ a bird in the trees.

flow	heard	bear	see
Ⓐ	Ⓑ	Ⓒ	Ⓓ

2. He will _____ some money.

earn	face	get	dear
Ⓐ	Ⓑ	Ⓒ	Ⓓ

3. She has a _____ necklace.

hear	grill	pearl	gold
Ⓐ	Ⓑ	Ⓒ	Ⓓ

4. In school we will _____ about leaves.

hill	gear	think	learn
Ⓐ	Ⓑ	Ⓒ	Ⓓ

STOP

DECODING/PHONICS

<u>**so**u**r**ce</u>

Sample

I am _____ in line.

peach	our	next	fourth
Ⓐ	Ⓑ	Ⓒ	Ⓓ

5. Let me _____ you a glass of water.

fur	bring	pour	dot
Ⓐ	Ⓑ	Ⓒ	Ⓓ

6. Our dog just had _____ puppies.

trust	four	out	some
Ⓐ	Ⓑ	Ⓒ	Ⓓ

7. They played a game at the tennis _____.

court	skunk	blur	club
Ⓐ	Ⓑ	Ⓒ	Ⓓ

8. That little stream is the _____ of a huge river.

beginning	source	clock	shout
Ⓐ	Ⓑ	Ⓒ	Ⓓ

STOP

Harcourt • Reading and Language Skills Assessment

DECODING/PHONICS: Abbreviations

Sample

I have a soccer game on <u>Thursday</u> afternoon.

Ths.   Thurs.   Tues.   Tu.
Ⓐ   Ⓑ   Ⓒ   Ⓓ

---

9. Luke's birthday is in <u>November</u>.

Nb.   Nbr.   Nov.   N.
Ⓐ   Ⓑ   Ⓒ   Ⓓ

10. Our new house is on Hunter <u>Avenue</u>.

An.   Ave.   Aug.   Apr.
Ⓐ   Ⓑ   Ⓒ   Ⓓ

11. Grandpa will come to see me this <u>Sunday</u>.

Sun.   Sept.   St.   Sat.
Ⓐ   Ⓑ   Ⓒ   Ⓓ

12. That basketball player is nearly seven <u>feet</u> tall.

f.   Feb.   Fri.   ft.
Ⓐ   Ⓑ   Ⓒ   Ⓓ

STOP

VOCABULARY: Synonyms

Sample

Small means _____.

hard	new	kind	little
Ⓐ	Ⓑ	Ⓒ	Ⓓ

13. Shouted means the same as _____.

walked	yelled	helped	started
Ⓐ	Ⓑ	Ⓒ	Ⓓ

14. Grinned means the same as _____.

smiled	answered	baked	fell
Ⓐ	Ⓑ	Ⓒ	Ⓓ

15. To be angry is to be _____.

hungry	mad	tired	full
Ⓐ	Ⓑ	Ⓒ	Ⓓ

16. Something enormous is very _____.

round	beautiful	large	able
Ⓐ	Ⓑ	Ⓒ	Ⓓ

STOP

Score _____

Just for You / Theme 2

Harcourt • Reading and Language Skills Assessment

COMPREHENSION: Sequence

Clang! Clang! Clang! The fire bell rang. The children in Mrs. Brown's class formed a line. They walked quickly, but they did not run or talk. Tina held the door open. Then she and Mrs. Brown joined the other children outside. "That was a very good fire drill," Mrs. Brown said. "Now that we are outside, let's play a game."

Sample

What happened first in the story?

Ⓐ The children talked.

Ⓑ The fire bell rang.

Ⓒ The children ran.

Ⓓ Mrs. Brown said something.

GO ON

COMPREHENSION: Sequence (continued)

17. What happened right after the fire bell rang?

Ⓐ The children played a game.

Ⓑ The children formed a line.

Ⓒ Mrs. Brown spoke to the class.

Ⓓ Mrs. Brown joined the children outside.

18. When did Tina hold the door open?

Ⓐ before the fire bell rang

Ⓑ before the children formed a line

Ⓒ after the children formed a line

Ⓓ after the children played a game

19. When did Tina and Mrs. Brown join the other children?

Ⓐ after they were all outside

Ⓑ after they played a game

Ⓒ before Tina held the door

Ⓓ before the children left the room

20. What happened last in the story?

Ⓐ The fire bell rang.

Ⓑ Tina and Mrs. Brown joined the children.

Ⓒ The children played a game outside.

Ⓓ The children went home.

STOP

LANGUAGE

Sample 1

Which word is a noun in this sentence?

Look at that silly monkey.

Ⓐ Look

Ⓑ silly

Ⓒ monkey

Sample 2

Which is the best way to write the underlined word in this sentence?

All of the <u>mans</u> had on jeans.

Ⓐ man

Ⓑ men

Ⓒ correct as is

21. Which word is a noun in this sentence?

The girls laughed and played.

Ⓐ girls

Ⓑ laughed

Ⓒ and

GO ON

LANGUAGE (continued)

22. Which word is a noun in this sentence?

My uncle is coming today.

(A) My

(B) uncle

(C) coming

23. Which is the best way to write the underlined word in this sentence?

All of the <u>child</u> won a prize.

(A) children

(B) childs

(C) correct as is

24. Which is the best way to write the underlined word in this sentence?

The five <u>box</u> are filled to the brim.

(A) boxs

(B) boxes

(C) correct as is

GO ON

Harcourt • Reading and Language Skills Assessment

LANGUAGE (continued)

25. Which is the best way to write the underlined word in this sentence?

There are seven new <u>bench</u> in the park.

Ⓐ benches

Ⓑ benchs

Ⓒ correct as is

26. Which is the best way to write the underlined words in this sentence?

Our family is moving to <u>dallas, texas</u>.

Ⓐ Dallas, Texas

Ⓑ dallas, Texas

Ⓒ correct as is

27. Which is the best way to write the underlined words in this sentence?

My neighbor is <u>Mr. Ben Sparks</u>.

Ⓐ mr. ben sparks

Ⓑ mr Ben Sparks

Ⓒ correct as is

GO ON ▶

LANGUAGE (continued)

28. Which is the best way to write the underlined words in this sentence?

Is your dentist <u>dr. jan merritt</u>?

Ⓐ Dr jan merritt

Ⓑ Dr. Jan Merritt

Ⓒ correct as is

29. Which is the best way to write the underlined words in this sentence?

Jess named her pet fish <u>flash and Fin</u>.

Ⓐ Flash and Fin

Ⓑ flash and fin

Ⓒ correct as is

30. Which is the best way to write the underlined words in this sentence?

<u>Miss susan barton</u> is our teacher.

Ⓐ Miss Susan Barton

Ⓑ miss susan barton

Ⓒ correct as is

STOP

Harcourt • Reading and Language Skills Assessment

· T R O P H I E S ·

Helping Hands / Theme 2
Reading and Language Skills Assessment

Harcourt

Orlando   Boston   Dallas   Chicago   San Diego

Part No. 9997-37713-3

ISBN 0-15-332175-X (Package of 12)

2-1

· T R O P H I E S ·

Reading and Language Skills Assessment Posttest

Just for You / Theme 2

Name _____ Date _____

SKILL AREA	Criterion Score	Pupil Score	Pupil Strength
DECODING/PHONICS			
R-controlled Vowels			
/ûr/*ear*	3/4	_____	_____
/ôr/*our*	3/4	_____	_____
Abbreviations	3/4	_____	_____
VOCABULARY			
Synonyms	3/4	_____	_____
COMPREHENSION			
Sequence	3/4	_____	_____
LANGUAGE	7/10	_____	_____
Nouns			
Plural Nouns			
Names of People			
Animals and Places			
TOTAL SCORE	22/30	_____	_____

Were accommodations made in administering this test? ❑ Yes ❑ No

Type of accommodations: _____

_____

DECODING/PHONICS

<u>ea</u>rth

Sample

We will _____ songs in music class.

year   rehearse   sing   radish
(A)   (B)   (C)   (D)

1. We planted seeds in the _____.

bear   match   earth   spring
(A)   (B)   (C)   (D)

2. Help me _____ for my lost puppy.

lamp   search   far   look
(A)   (B)   (C)   (D)

3. We will go to bed _____.

every   star   now   early
(A)   (B)   (C)   (D)

4. My sister will _____ to ride a bike.

learn   have   most   team
(A)   (B)   (C)   (D)

STOP

DECODING/PHONICS

<u>sour</u>ce

Sample

I am _____ in line.

peach	our	next	fourth
Ⓐ	Ⓑ	Ⓒ	Ⓓ

---

5. The king was in his _____.

dust	court	shout	throne
Ⓐ	Ⓑ	Ⓒ	Ⓓ

6. I _____ some milk on my cereal.

burn	broke	put	poured
Ⓐ	Ⓑ	Ⓒ	Ⓓ

7. Mom will take a _____ in Spanish.

course	class	found	cost
Ⓐ	Ⓑ	Ⓒ	Ⓓ

8. My older brother is _____.

churn	cling	fourteen	tall
Ⓐ	Ⓑ	Ⓒ	Ⓓ

STOP

Score _____ *Just for You* / Theme 2

Harcourt • Reading and Language Skills Assessment

DECODING/PHONICS: Abbreviations

Sample

I have a soccer game on <u>Thursday</u> afternoon.

Ths.   Thurs.   Tues.   Tu.
Ⓐ   Ⓑ   Ⓒ   Ⓓ

9. <u>January</u> 1 is the first day of the new year.

Jay.   Jan.   Jn.   Jr.
Ⓐ   Ⓑ   Ⓒ   Ⓓ

10. My desk is 18 <u>inches</u> wide.

is.   I.   in.   ichs.
Ⓐ   Ⓑ   Ⓒ   Ⓓ

11. Our class will go to the library on <u>Tuesday</u>.

Tusd.   Ty.   Thurs.   Tues.
Ⓐ   Ⓑ   Ⓒ   Ⓓ

12. There is a new toy store on Collins <u>Drive</u>.

Dr.   Dec.   Dve.   Dv.
Ⓐ   Ⓑ   Ⓒ   Ⓓ

STOP

VOCABULARY: Synonyms

Sample

Small means _____.

hard   new   kind   little
Ⓐ   Ⓑ   Ⓒ   Ⓓ

---

13. Arrived means the same as _____.

came   turned   owned   locked
Ⓐ   Ⓑ   Ⓒ   Ⓓ

14. Nearly means the same as _____.

fresh   almost   old   large
Ⓐ   Ⓑ   Ⓒ   Ⓓ

15. To be sad is to be _____.

cold   eager   tall   unhappy
Ⓐ   Ⓑ   Ⓒ   Ⓓ

16. Something beautiful is very _____.

square   thick   pretty   loud
Ⓐ   Ⓑ   Ⓒ   Ⓓ

STOP

Score _____   *Just for You* / Theme 2

Harcourt • Reading and Language Skills Assessment

COMPREHENSION: Sequence

Lightning flashed outside. Then Maria heard a loud crash of thunder. She ran to the window and looked out. It was raining hard. "Mom," she called, "come quick! The car windows are open. Everything will get wet." Her mom rushed from the kitchen. "Maria," she said, "help me find the umbrella. Hurry!" They began to look.

Just then, they heard someone at the door. Maria's mom opened it. Their neighbor, Alex, stood in the doorway. He was soaking wet. Alex wiped the rain from his eyes and said, "Hello, Mrs. Garza. Your car windows were down, so I rolled them up."

Sample

What happened first in the story?

Ⓐ Maria heard thunder.

Ⓑ Lightning flashed.

Ⓒ Mom opened the door.

Ⓓ Alex wiped rain from his eyes.

GO ON

COMPREHENSION: Sequence (continued)

17. What happened just before Maria ran to the window?

    (A) She heard someone at the door.

    (B) She looked for an umbrella.

    (C) She heard a loud crash of thunder.

    (D) She told Mom the windows were open.

18. When did Maria's mother rush from the kitchen?

    (A) before Maria looked out the window

    (B) before the rain started falling

    (C) after Alex came to the door

    (D) after Maria told her about the car windows

19. When did Maria and her mother hear someone at the door?

    (A) after they began to look for the umbrella

    (B) after Alex wiped rain from his eyes

    (C) before Maria ran to the window

    (D) before they heard thunder

20. What happened last in the story?

    (A) Maria looked out the window.

    (B) Maria's mother opened the door.

    (C) Alex said he rolled up the windows.

    (D) Alex stood in the doorway.

STOP

Harcourt • Reading and Language Skills Assessment

LANGUAGE

Sample 1

Which word is a noun in this sentence?

Look at that silly monkey.

(A) Look

(B) silly

(C) monkey

Sample 2

Which is the best way to write the underlined word in this sentence?

All of the <u>mans</u> had on jeans.

(A) man

(B) men

(C) correct as is

21. Which word is a noun in this sentence?

My friend will visit tomorrow.

(A) My

(B) friend

(C) visit

GO ON

LANGUAGE (continued)

22. Which word is a noun in this sentence?

The dancer twirled and leaped.

Ⓐ dancer

Ⓑ twirled

Ⓒ leaped

23. Which is the best way to write the underlined word in this sentence?

Many <u>man</u> were on the team.

Ⓐ men

Ⓑ mans

Ⓒ correct as is

24. Which is the best way to write the underlined word in this sentence?

We saw many <u>shell</u> at the beach.

Ⓐ shelles

Ⓑ shells

Ⓒ correct as is

GO ON

Harcourt • Reading and Language Skills Assessment

LANGUAGE (continued)

25. Which is the best way to write the underlined word in this sentence?

I washed all the <u>dishes</u>.

Ⓐ dish

Ⓑ dishs

Ⓒ correct as is

26. Which is the best way to write the underlined words in this sentence?

My best friends are <u>sara and Matt</u>.

Ⓐ Sara and Matt

Ⓑ sara and matt

Ⓒ correct as is

27. Which is the best way to write the underlined words in this sentence?

Thank you for the cookies, <u>mrs. Chan</u>.

Ⓐ mrs chan

Ⓑ Mrs. Chan

Ⓒ correct as is

GO ON ▶

LANGUAGE (continued)

28. Which is the best way to write the underlined words in this sentence?

My dogs are named <u>skippy and jet</u>.

Ⓐ Skippy and Jet

Ⓑ skippy and Jet

Ⓒ correct as is

29. Which is the best way to write the underlined words in this sentence?

Have you ever been to <u>Park City</u>?

Ⓐ park City

Ⓑ park city

Ⓒ correct as is

30. Which is the best way to write the underlined words in this sentence?

The flowers are blooming on <u>apple Blossom drive</u>.

Ⓐ apple blossom drive

Ⓑ Apple Blossom Drive

Ⓒ correct as is

STOP

Score _____

Harcourt • Reading and Language Skills Assessment

• T R O P H I E S •

Helping Hands / Theme 2
Reading and Language Skills Assessment

Harcourt

Orlando   Boston   Dallas   Chicago   San Diego

Part No. 9997-37710-9

ISBN 0-15-332175-X (Package of 12)

2-1

TROPHIES

Reading and Language Skills Assessment Pretest

Just for You / Theme 3

Name _____ Date _____

SKILL AREA	Criterion Score	Pupil Score	Pupil Strength
DECODING/PHONICS			
R-controlled Vowels /ir/*ear, eer*	3/4	_____	_____
Vowel Digraphs /$\overline{oo}$/*oo*	3/4	_____	_____
Inflectional Endings -*s*, -*es*, -*ies*, (*y* to *i*)	3/4	_____	_____
COMPREHENSION	3/4		
Interpret Information: Charts, Graphs, Diagrams		_____	_____
Details	3/4	_____	_____
Make Inferences	3/4	_____	_____
Follow Two-Step Written Directions	3/4	_____	_____
LANGUAGE	7/10	_____	_____
Names of Days			
Names of Months			
Names of Holidays			
Showing Ownership			
TOTAL SCORE	28/38	_____	_____

Were accommodations made in administering this test? ☐ Yes ☐ No

Type of accommodations: _____

_____

Printed in the United States of America

ISBN 0-15-332175-X

6 7 8 9 10   170   10 09 08 07 06 05 04

DECODING/PHONICS

app**ear**   sn**eer**

Sample

Did you _____ Jed come into the house?

steam	let	hear	back
Ⓐ	Ⓑ	Ⓒ	Ⓓ

1. We took flowers to _____ our friend.

pack	help	cheer	bear
Ⓐ	Ⓑ	Ⓒ	Ⓓ

2. Do not go far, because I want you to stay _____ me.

near	cheap	beside	test
Ⓐ	Ⓑ	Ⓒ	Ⓓ

3. My uncle let me _____ the boat when we went out on the lake.

steer	shave	earth	turn
Ⓐ	Ⓑ	Ⓒ	Ⓓ

4. The water looks clean and _____.

blue	earn	less	clear
Ⓐ	Ⓑ	Ⓒ	Ⓓ

STOP

DECODING/PHONICS

<u>soo</u>n

Sample

What kind of _____ do you like to eat?

took   kick   food   cake

Ⓐ   Ⓑ   Ⓒ   Ⓓ

5. The _____ of the tree went down deep in the dirt.

fit   roots   look   seeds

Ⓐ   Ⓑ   Ⓒ   Ⓓ

6. That _____ has big antlers on his head.

moose   book   ship   deer

Ⓐ   Ⓑ   Ⓒ   Ⓓ

7. The _____ is shining brightly in the sky.

rock   bike   sun   moon

Ⓐ   Ⓑ   Ⓒ   Ⓓ

8. I need a _____ to eat my cereal.

mop   tire   spoon   bowl

Ⓐ   Ⓑ   Ⓒ   Ⓓ

STOP

Harcourt • Reading and Language Skills Assessment

DECODING/PHONICS

Sample

I have lived in three different _____.

city   cityes   cities   citys
Ⓐ   Ⓑ   Ⓒ   Ⓓ

---

9. I saw a mother bird with three little _____.

babyes   babies   baby   babys
Ⓐ   Ⓑ   Ⓒ   Ⓓ

10. She will clean all the _____.

windows   window   windowes   windowies
Ⓐ   Ⓑ   Ⓒ   Ⓓ

11. Five _____ make one nickel.

penny   pennys   pennyes   pennies
Ⓐ   Ⓑ   Ⓒ   Ⓓ

12. I made two _____, and they both came true.

wishs   wishes   wishies   wish
Ⓐ   Ⓑ   Ⓒ   Ⓓ

STOP

COMPREHENSION: Interpret Information

Sample

Mrs. Clarke's class is studying pets. They made a graph to show the kinds of pets they have.

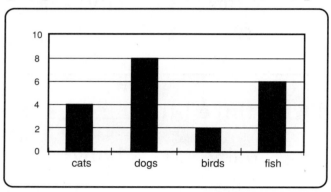

Which pet is **not** on the graph?

Ⓐ birds

Ⓑ cats

Ⓒ fish

Ⓓ hamsters

GO ON

COMPREHENSION: Interpret Information (continued)

13. How many children have cats as pets?

Ⓐ 2

Ⓑ 4

Ⓒ 6

Ⓓ 8

14. How many children have birds as pets?

Ⓐ 2

Ⓑ 4

Ⓒ 6

Ⓓ 8

15. How many children have fish as pets?

Ⓐ 2

Ⓑ 4

Ⓒ 6

Ⓓ 8

16. Which pet do most of the children have?

Ⓐ cats

Ⓑ dogs

Ⓒ birds

Ⓓ fish

STOP

COMPREHENSION: Details

Bats are strange animals. Bats are quite small and look a little like a mouse with wings. The heads of some bats look like little bulldogs, or like bears with long teeth. Other kinds of bats have long noses. Bats help people because they eat insects. They also help make new plants by carrying pollen from one flower to another. One of the strangest things about bats is how they sleep. They hang upside down when they sleep. They also sleep during the day! Many people are afraid of bats because they think that bats bite. Only a sick bat will bite a person. If you leave bats alone, they will leave you alone.

Sample

Many people are afraid that bats will _____.

(A) bite them

(B) eat their food

(C) eat their flowers

(D) make them sick

17. Bats are about the size of a _____.

(A) cat

(B) bear

(C) mouse

(D) man

GO ON

Harcourt • Reading and Language Skills Assessment

COMPREHENSION: Details (continued)

18. Bats help people because they _____.

Ⓐ have long teeth

Ⓑ eat insects

Ⓒ look like little bulldogs

Ⓓ have long noses

19. The way bats sleep is strange because they _____.

Ⓐ sleep a long time

Ⓑ do not need much sleep

Ⓒ sleep with their eyes open

Ⓓ sleep upside down

20. What do bats do during the day?

Ⓐ sleep

Ⓑ eat insects

Ⓒ bite people

Ⓓ carry pollen

STOP

Harcourt • Reading and Language Skills Assessment

COMPREHENSION: Make Inferences

Tony had a warm bath. After that, he brushed his teeth. Then he went into his bedroom, got in bed, and turned off the light. He put his head on the soft pillow and closed his eyes.

Sample

What is Tony starting to do?

Ⓐ play a game

Ⓑ go to sleep

Ⓒ read a book

Ⓓ write a letter

GO ON

Just for You / Theme 3

COMPREHENSION: Make Inferences (continued)

Gina's mother has a friend named Miss Katy. Miss Katy paints pictures of big swirls and splashes in bright colors. Gina loves Miss Katy's house. It is full of paintings and statues and pots made of clay. Miss Katy made many of the clay pots. Miss Katy also has a little black dog named Sammy. Sammy barks and barks when anyone comes into the house. Once a month, Gina and her mother go to visit Miss Katy. They like to see her new paintings and pots. Miss Katy always serves them little square cakes covered with pink frosting. Sammy sits up and barks until Gina gives him a tiny piece.

21. You can tell that Miss Katy is _____.

Ⓐ a teacher

Ⓑ an artist

Ⓒ a police officer

Ⓓ a doctor

22. Sammy sits up because he wants to _____ .

Ⓐ play with Gloria

Ⓑ eat cake

Ⓒ come inside

Ⓓ scare Gina

GO ON

Harcourt • Reading and Language Skills Assessment

COMPREHENSION: Make Inferences (continued)

Mr. Solis watched the teacher put on his skis. Mr. Solis looked down at his own feet. They were snug and warm in bright blue ski boots. He set his skis on the snowy ground and tried to put them on. It wasn't easy. Mr. Solis felt clumsy. "Maybe I am too old to learn this," he thought. Then he tried again and this time he made it. He looked at the teacher and smiled. The teacher said, "Are you ready?" Mr. Solis looked down at the beautiful white snow on the slopes below him. He took a deep breath. "Ready," he said.

23. Where does this story take place?

Ⓐ on a mountain

Ⓑ in Mr. Solis's house

Ⓒ on a frozen pond

Ⓓ in a shoe store

24. What is Mr. Solis learning to do?

Ⓐ shine boots

Ⓑ teach a class

Ⓒ shovel snow

Ⓓ ski

STOP

COMPREHENSION: Follow Two-Step Written Directions

How to Make a Banana Split

Here is what you need to make a banana split:

ice cream

a banana

1. Peel a banana. Then cut it in half and put it in a bowl.

2. Put two scoops of ice cream on top of the banana.

Sample

What do you do first to make a banana split?

Ⓐ Put ice cream on the banana.

Ⓑ Peel a banana.

Ⓒ Cut the banana in half.

Ⓓ Put the banana in a bowl.

GO ON

COMPREHENSION: Follow Two-Step Written Directions (continued)

Rosa and her mother are walking to school together. Here are the steps to get there:

1. Walk down King Street until you get to a stop sign.

2. Turn right onto Vine Street. Walk only one block. The school is at the end of Vine Street. It has a flag in front of it. If you see a sign for Mill Street, you have walked too far.

25. At the stop sign, Rosa and her mother should _____.

Ⓐ go straight

Ⓑ turn left

Ⓒ turn right

Ⓓ turn around

GO ON

COMPREHENSION: Follow Two-Step Written Directions (continued)

26. What street is the school on?

Ⓐ King

Ⓑ Vine

Ⓒ Flag

Ⓓ Mill

27. How many blocks should Rosa and her mother walk on Vine Street?

Ⓐ one

Ⓑ two

Ⓒ three

Ⓓ four

28. What is in front of the school?

Ⓐ a king

Ⓑ a vine

Ⓒ a flag

Ⓓ a mill

STOP

LANGUAGE

> **Sample**
>
> We are making different foods for <u>thanksgiving day</u>.
>
> Ⓐ thanksgiving Day
>
> Ⓑ Thanksgiving Day
>
> Ⓒ correct as is

29. Our family will be in California from <u>june until July</u>.

   Ⓐ june until july

   Ⓑ June until July

   Ⓒ correct as is

30. What will you do on <u>New Year's Day</u>?

   Ⓐ New year's day

   Ⓑ new year's day

   Ⓒ correct as is

31. We will be out of town on <u>saturday and sunday</u>.

   Ⓐ Saturday and Sunday

   Ⓑ saturday and Sunday

   Ⓒ correct as is

GO ON

LANGUAGE (continued)

32. We will watch fireworks on the <u>fourth of july</u>.

    Ⓐ fourth of July

    Ⓑ Fourth of July

    Ⓒ correct as is

33. <u>The tail of the cat</u> is long.

    Ⓐ The cats tail

    Ⓑ The cat tail's

    Ⓒ The cat's tail

34. I rode to school on <u>the bike of my brother</u>.

    Ⓐ my brother bike's

    Ⓑ my brother's bike

    Ⓒ my brothers bike

35. I go to dance class on <u>tuesday and Thursday</u>.

    Ⓐ Tuesday and Thursday

    Ⓑ Tuesday and thursday

    Ⓒ correct as is

GO ON

LANGUAGE (continued)

36. It is cold here from <u>December through march.</u>

  Ⓐ december through march

  Ⓑ December through March

  Ⓒ correct as is

37. Our class will put on a play on <u>Thursday, april 12.</u>

  Ⓐ Thursday, April 12

  Ⓑ thursday, april 12

  Ⓒ correct as is

38. <u>The mother of my friend</u> says I may eat supper with them.

  Ⓐ My friends mother

  Ⓑ My friend mother's

  Ⓒ My friend's mother

STOP

· TROPHIES ·

Our World / Theme 3
Reading and Language Skills Assessment

Harcourt

Orlando   Boston   Dallas   Chicago   San Diego

Part No. 9997-37714-1

ISBN 0-15-332175-X (Package of 12)

2-3

TROPHIES

Reading and Language Skills Assessment Posttest

Just for You / Theme 3

Name_____ Date_____

SKILL AREA	Criterion Score	Pupil Score	Pupil Strength
DECODING/PHONICS			
R-controlled Vowels /ir/*ear, eer*	3/4	_____	_____
Vowel Digraphs /o͞o/*oo*	3/4	_____	_____
Inflectional Endings -*s*, -*es*, -*ies*, (*y* to *i*)	3/4	_____	_____
COMPREHENSION			
Interpret Information: Charts, Graphs, Diagrams	3/4	_____	_____
Details	3/4	_____	_____
Make Inferences	3/4	_____	_____
Follow Two-Step Written Directions	3/4	_____	_____
LANGUAGE	7/10	_____	_____
Names of Days			
Names of Months			
Names of Holidays			
Showing Ownership			
TOTAL SCORE	28/38	_____	_____

Were accommodations made in administering this test? ☐ Yes ☐ No

Type of accommodations: _____

_____

Printed in the United States of America

ISBN 0-15-332175-X

6 7 8 9 10   170   10 09 08 07 06 05 04

DECODING/PHONICS

appear **sneer**

Sample

Did you _____ Jed come into the house?

steam	let	hear	back
Ⓐ	Ⓑ	Ⓒ	Ⓓ

1. I will be eight next _____.

wash	year	month	fern
Ⓐ	Ⓑ	Ⓒ	Ⓓ

2. The _____ cut trees to build log cabins.

pioneers	silks	learn	people
Ⓐ	Ⓑ	Ⓒ	Ⓓ

3. That man has a thick _____.

beat	beard	song	belt
Ⓐ	Ⓑ	Ⓒ	Ⓓ

4. The mother _____ and her baby were sleeping.

grass	search	deer	rabbit
Ⓐ	Ⓑ	Ⓒ	Ⓓ

STOP

DECODING/PHONICS

<u>soo</u>n

Sample

What kind of _____ do you like to eat?

took	kick	food	cake
Ⓐ	Ⓑ	Ⓒ	Ⓓ

5. My little sister likes to _____ her new horn.

blush	toot	cot	blow
Ⓐ	Ⓑ	Ⓒ	Ⓓ

6. I stepped in a puddle and got mud on my _____.

boots	noise	socks	shout
Ⓐ	Ⓑ	Ⓒ	Ⓓ

7. Mom will _____ the seeds out of the pumpkin.

hope	meet	scoop	take
Ⓐ	Ⓑ	Ⓒ	Ⓓ

8. The flowers have just started to _____.

run	crash	grow	bloom
Ⓐ	Ⓑ	Ⓒ	Ⓓ

STOP

Harcourt • Reading and Language Skills Assessment

DECODING/PHONICS

Sample

I have lived in three different _____.

city
(A)

cityes
(B)

cities
(C)

citys
(D)

---

9. She has many different _____.

hobby
(A)

hobbys
(B)

hobbies
(C)

hobbyes
(D)

10. The children got into three _____ to play a game.

groups
(A)

groupes
(B)

group
(C)

groupies
(D)

11. My dog just had three _____.

puppy
(A)

puppys
(B)

puppyes
(C)

puppies
(D)

12. My sister helped Mom wash all the _____.

dishs
(A)

dishes
(B)

dishies
(C)

dish
(D)

STOP

COMPREHENSION: Interpret Information

Stacy's class needed money for a class trip. They decided to have a bake sale at school. The children brought baked goods from home. Stacy's teacher made this sign to put up.

apple pie	**$1.00**
cheesecake	**75¢**
cookie	**10¢**
cupcake	**50¢**
brownie	**75¢**

Sample

How much does cheesecake cost?

Ⓐ 10¢

Ⓑ 50¢

Ⓒ 75¢

Ⓓ $1.00

GO ON

Just for You / Theme 3

COMPREHENSION: Interpret Information (continued)

13. How much does a cupcake cost?

Ⓐ 10¢

Ⓑ 50¢

Ⓒ 75¢

Ⓓ $1.00

14. What costs the same as a brownie?

Ⓐ apple pie

Ⓑ cheesecake

Ⓒ cookie

Ⓓ cupcake

15. Which one costs the most?

Ⓐ apple pie

Ⓑ cheesecake

Ⓒ cookie

Ⓓ cupcake

16. Which costs the least?

Ⓐ apple pie

Ⓑ cupcake

Ⓒ brownie

Ⓓ cookie

STOP

COMPREHENSION: Details

Dan teaches boys and girls how to play baseball. He teaches them to run fast, to throw the ball, and to bat. He is best at teaching them how to bat. Dan shows the children where to stand. "Your feet should be sixteen inches from the home plate," he says. "Stand evenly on both feet in the batter's box. When the pitcher throws the ball, move your body." He says, "Lean back on your back foot. This helps you get ready to swing." Next, Dan shows how to swing hard. "Turn your body when you swing," says Dan. "Don't close your eyes. You will get a hit. You might even get a home run!"

Sample

What does Dan teach children to play?

Ⓐ soccer

Ⓑ tennis

Ⓒ baseball

Ⓓ basketball

17. Dan is best at teaching children how to _____.

Ⓐ run

Ⓑ throw

Ⓒ bat

Ⓓ stand

GO ON

COMPREHENSION: Details (continued)

18. When you bat, you should put your feet sixteen inches from _____.

   Ⓐ the batter's box

   Ⓑ the home plate

   Ⓒ the catcher

   Ⓓ the pitcher

19. What helps you get ready to swing the bat?

   Ⓐ listening to the coach

   Ⓑ watching the catcher

   Ⓒ keeping your feet straight

   Ⓓ leaning on your back foot

20. You will swing hard if you _____.

   Ⓐ stand on both feet

   Ⓑ close your eyes

   Ⓒ turn your body

   Ⓓ throw the bat

STOP

COMPREHENSION: Make Inferences

Tony had a warm bath. After that, he brushed his teeth. Then he went into his bedroom, got in bed, and turned off the light. He put his head on the soft pillow and closed his eyes.

Sample

What is Tony starting to do?

Ⓐ play a game

Ⓑ go to sleep

Ⓒ read a book

Ⓓ write a letter

GO ON

Harcourt • Reading and Language Skills Assessment

COMPREHENSION: Make Inferences (continued)

Lorenzo wanted a pet. His mother said that a cat or a dog would be too big for their apartment. She said he could get a small pet. At the pet store, Lorenzo saw cats, dogs, and even a huge snake. Then he saw just the right pet for him. Lorenzo bought the pet and named him Willy.

Lorenzo got a little cage for Willy. Now he makes sure Willy has fresh food and water each day. He put a bowl and a special water bottle inside the cage. He also bought a little wheel for Willy to run on. Willy climbs inside the wheel and runs and runs. Lorenzo and his mother laugh when they see Willy running around and around.

21. What pet did Lorenzo buy?
    Ⓐ cat
    Ⓑ dog
    Ⓒ hamster
    Ⓓ snake

22. What can you tell about Lorenzo?
    Ⓐ He takes good care of a pet.
    Ⓑ He makes good grades in school.
    Ⓒ He has many friends.
    Ⓓ He can do tricks.

GO ON

Harcourt • Reading and Language Skills Assessment

COMPREHENSION: Make Inferences (continued)

Mara looked at her tooth in the mirror. It was loose. She touched it, and it wiggled. "Let me touch it," her brother said.

"Oh, no! You'll pull it," Mara said.

Later that day, all Mara's classmates wanted to wiggle her tooth. They promised not to pull it, but she was afraid, so she said no. As the day went on, the tooth just got looser.

The next morning, Mara woke up. Her tooth was missing. "Look under your pillow and under the sheets," her mother said.

23. Where was Mara when the children wanted to wiggle her tooth?

Ⓐ in bed

Ⓑ at school

Ⓒ in her bathroom

Ⓓ in her mother's room

24. What probably happened to Mara's tooth?

Ⓐ A dentist took it out.

Ⓑ Her brother pulled it out.

Ⓒ It fell out when she was asleep.

Ⓓ Her mother pulled it out.

STOP

COMPREHENSION: Follow Two-Step Written Directions

How to Make a Banana Split

Here is what you need to make a banana split:

ice cream

a banana

1. Peel a banana. Then cut it in half and put it in a bowl.

2. Put two scoops of ice cream on top of the banana.

Sample

What do you do first to make a banana split?

Ⓐ Put ice cream on the banana.

Ⓑ Peel a banana.

Ⓒ Cut the banana in half.

Ⓓ Put the banana in a bowl.

GO ON

COMPREHENSION: Follow Two-Step Written Directions (continued)

How to Make Lemonade

First, have a grown-up squeeze the juice from several lemons.

1. Mix the lemon juice with water.

2. Add sugar until the lemonade is sweet enough.

25. What is the first thing you do to make lemonade?

   (A) Add sugar.

   (B) Mix the lemon juice with water.

   (C) Have a grown-up squeeze the lemons.

   (D) Add ice cubes.

26. What does step 1 say to mix with the lemon juice?

   (A) water

   (B) ice

   (C) sugar

   (D) lemons

GO ON

COMPREHENSION: Follow Two-Step Written Directions (continued)

27. What must be added in step 2?

  Ⓐ lemons

  Ⓑ water

  Ⓒ ice

  Ⓓ sugar

28. Based on the last step, why should you add sugar?

  Ⓐ to make the lemonade cold

  Ⓑ to make the lemonade sweet

  Ⓒ to make the lemonade thick

  Ⓓ to make the lemonade yellow

STOP

Harcourt • Reading and Language Skills Assessment

LANGUAGE

Sample

We are making different foods for <u>thanksgiving day</u>.

Ⓐ thanksgiving Day

Ⓑ Thanksgiving Day

Ⓒ correct as is

---

29. Were you born in <u>january or february</u>?

Ⓐ January or February

Ⓑ january or February

Ⓒ correct as is

30. Our teacher gave us cards on <u>valentine's Day</u>.

Ⓐ valentine's day

Ⓑ Valentine's Day

Ⓒ correct as is

31. We have music class on <u>wednesday and friday</u>.

Ⓐ Wednesday and Friday

Ⓑ Wednesday and friday

Ⓒ correct as is

GO ON ➤

Harcourt • Reading and Language Skills Assessment

LANGUAGE (continued)

32. We will plant a tree on <u>Arbor Day</u> .

Ⓐ arbor day

Ⓑ arbor Day

Ⓒ correct as is

33. <u>The smile of the baby</u> is sweet.

Ⓐ The babys smile

Ⓑ The baby's smile

Ⓒ The baby smile's

34. <u>The bark of that dog</u> is very loud.

Ⓐ That dog bark's

Ⓑ That dogs bark

Ⓒ That dog's bark

35. May I visit you on <u>monday or tuesday</u>?

Ⓐ Monday or tuesday

Ⓑ Monday or Tuesday

Ⓒ correct as is

GO ON

LANGUAGE (continued)

36. Our class will have a picnic in <u>april or May</u>.

    Ⓐ April or May

    Ⓑ april or may

    Ⓒ correct as is

37. <u>The song of the bird</u> sounds cheerful.

    Ⓐ The bird song's

    Ⓑ The bird's song

    Ⓒ The birds song

38. Our family will go to the beach on <u>Friday, july 27</u>.

    Ⓐ friday, july 27

    Ⓑ Friday, July 27

    Ⓒ correct as is

STOP

Our World / Theme 3
Reading and Language Skills Assessment

Harcourt

Orlando   Boston   Dallas   Chicago   San Diego

Part No. 9997-37711-7

ISBN 0-15-332175-X (Package of 12)

2-1

· T R O P H I E S ·

Mid-Year Reading and Language Skills Assessment

Just for You / Themes 1, 2, 3

Name_____ Date_____

SKILL AREA	Criterion Score	Pupil Score	Comments
DECODING/PHONICS	13/18	_____	_____
VOCABULARY	3/4	_____	_____
COMPREHENSION	13/18	_____	_____
LANGUAGE	7/10	_____	_____
TOTAL SCORE	36/50	_____	_____

Were accommodations made in administering this test?   ❑ Yes   ❑ No

Type of accommodations: _____

_____

DECODING/PHONICS

earth

Sample

We will _____ songs in music class.

year	rehearse	sing	radish
Ⓐ	Ⓑ	Ⓒ	Ⓓ

1. Bill will _____ some money by walking a dog.

check	earn	make	hear
Ⓐ	Ⓑ	Ⓒ	Ⓓ

2. Please help me _____ for my lost watch.

trash	near	look	search
Ⓐ	Ⓑ	Ⓒ	Ⓓ

3. I _____ some news.

heard	dear	know	cold
Ⓐ	Ⓑ	Ⓒ	Ⓓ

STOP

DECODING/PHONICS (continued)

source

Sample

I am _____ in line.

peach	our	next	fourth
Ⓐ	Ⓑ	Ⓒ	Ⓓ

---

4. Will you _____ me a glass of milk?

fur	get	pour	sung
Ⓐ	Ⓑ	Ⓒ	Ⓓ

5. I got _____ gifts today.

must	out	some	four
Ⓐ	Ⓑ	Ⓒ	Ⓓ

6. The judge is in his _____.

court	eagle	room	burn
Ⓐ	Ⓑ	Ⓒ	Ⓓ

STOP

Harcourt • Reading and Language Skills Assessment

DECODING/PHONICS (continued)

Sample

I have a soccer game on <u>Thursday</u> afternoon.

Ths.   Thurs.   Tues.   Tu.

Ⓐ   Ⓑ   Ⓒ   Ⓓ

---

7. I was born in <u>January</u>.

Jnr.   Jan.   Jy.   J.

Ⓐ   Ⓑ   Ⓒ   Ⓓ

8. Which way is it to Mills <u>Avenue</u>?

An.   Ave.   Aug.   Apr.

Ⓐ   Ⓑ   Ⓒ   Ⓓ

9. That worm is three <u>inches</u> long.

is.   I.   in.   ichs.

Ⓐ   Ⓑ   Ⓒ   Ⓓ

STOP

DECODING/PHONICS (continued)

---

app<u>ear</u>   **sn<u>eer</u>**

Sample

Did you _____ Jed come into the house?

steam	let	hear	back
Ⓐ	Ⓑ	Ⓒ	Ⓓ

---

10. I have a pain in my _____.

tack	ear	neck	pear
Ⓐ	Ⓑ	Ⓒ	Ⓓ

11. Does Mr. Smith live _____?

nearby	chest	far	learn
Ⓐ	Ⓑ	Ⓒ	Ⓓ

12. Dad will _____ the car while Mom reads the map.

peep	behave	steer	drive
Ⓐ	Ⓑ	Ⓒ	Ⓓ

STOP

Harcourt • Reading and Language Skills Assessment

DECODING/PHONICS (continued)

___
soon

Sample

What kind of _____ do you like to eat?

took   kick   food   cake
Ⓐ   Ⓑ   Ⓒ   Ⓓ

13. Get a _____ and help me clean the floor.

look   bright   broom   mop
Ⓐ   Ⓑ   Ⓒ   Ⓓ

14. Come into my _____.

crow   room   mop   house
Ⓐ   Ⓑ   Ⓒ   Ⓓ

15. Please hand me a _____ to eat with.

sock   like   fork   spoon
Ⓐ   Ⓑ   Ⓒ   Ⓓ

STOP

DECODING/PHONICS (continued)

Sample

I have lived in three different _____.

city   cityes   cities   citys

Ⓐ   Ⓑ   Ⓒ   Ⓓ

16. The baby _____ when she is hungry.

cryes   cries   cry   crys

Ⓐ   Ⓑ   Ⓒ   Ⓓ

17. I ate the whole bowl of _____.

cherries   cherry   cherryes   cherrys

Ⓐ   Ⓑ   Ⓒ   Ⓓ

18. Did you pack both our _____?

lunchies   lunchs   lunch   lunches

Ⓐ   Ⓑ   Ⓒ   Ⓓ

STOP

VOCABULARY

Sample

Small means _____.

Ⓐ hard

Ⓑ new

Ⓒ kind

Ⓓ little

---

19. To be cozy means to be _____.

Ⓐ thin

Ⓑ snug

Ⓒ hard

Ⓓ cold

20. Arrived means the same as _____.

Ⓐ came

Ⓑ called

Ⓒ knew

Ⓓ cleaned

GO ON ▶

VOCABULARY (continued)

21. <u>Raced</u> means the same as _____.

   Ⓐ told

   Ⓑ ran

   Ⓒ thought

   Ⓓ wanted

22. <u>Smeared</u> means the same as _____.

   Ⓐ answered

   Ⓑ gave

   Ⓒ spread

   Ⓓ sounded

STOP

Score_____

Harcourt • Reading and Language Skills Assessment

COMPREHENSION

> Sal and Jeff were talking. They could not decide what to do. They had all afternoon to play, but they wanted to do different things. Sal said, "I want to run around outside. I want to play baseball."
>
> Jeff said, "I want to stay inside. I want to work a puzzle."
>
> Both boys wanted to have some fun.
>
> "Let's work a puzzle," Jeff said.
>
> "No, let's play baseball," Sal said.
>
> Then Jeff's big sister Ann came into the room. She had been listening. Ann said, "Why don't you go over to Sal's house? You can play baseball there for a while. After you play ball, you can come back here and work a puzzle together."
>
> "Good idea!" Sal and Jeff said. "Let's go!" They ran out the door to have fun.

Sample

What are Sal and Jeff doing at the beginning of the story?

(A) playing ball

(B) working a puzzle

(C) talking about what to do

(D) playing a game with Ann

GO ON

COMPREHENSION (continued)

23. Jeff and Sal **both** want to _____.

(A) work puzzles

(B) have fun

(C) play outside

(D) play with Ann

24. What happens **after** Ann tells the boys her idea?

(A) Ann comes into the room.

(B) Jeff says he wants to stay inside.

(C) The boys run out the door.

(D) The boys talk about what to do for fun.

25. What do Sal and Jeff decide to do?

(A) They will just play baseball.

(B) They will just work a puzzle.

(C) They will play ball and work a puzzle.

(D) They will find a different game they both like.

26. What can you tell about Jeff and Sal?

(A) They like to spend time together.

(B) They make good grades in school.

(C) They help do chores at home.

(D) They are the same size.

GO ON

Harcourt • Reading and Language Skills Assessment

COMPREHENSION (continued)

> You should check your home inside and out to be sure it is safe from fire. See that matches are put away out of the reach of small children. Check to see that your toaster is unplugged when it is not being used. If you find any rags with oil or paint on them, clean them or throw them away in a safe place. Make sure there is no trash left lying around that might catch on fire.

27. What is this story mostly about?

(A) See that matches are put away out of the reach of small children.

(B) Check to see that your toaster is unplugged when it is not being used.

(C) Make sure there is no trash left lying around that might catch on fire.

(D) You should check your home inside and out to be sure it is safe from fire.

28. What does the story say you should do with rags that have oil on them?

(A) Clean them or throw them away.

(B) Use them to clean the toaster.

(C) Keep them to use again.

(D) Give them to a neighbor.

GO ON

COMPREHENSION (continued)

We have learned that to stay well and to think clearly, you need to get enough sleep. Different people have different sleep needs. Some people may need only five or six hours of sleep each night. Other people may need eight hours or more. You should be sure to get as much sleep as you need each night. It could even help you do better work in school.

29. What is this story mostly about?

(A) Some people may need only five or six hours of sleep each night.

(B) Other people may need eight hours or more.

(C) We have learned that to stay well and to think clearly, you need to get enough sleep.

(D) It could even help you do better work in school.

30. How much sleep should you get each night?

(A) five hours a night

(B) six hours a night

(C) eight hours or more a night

(D) different hours for different people

GO ON

Harcourt • Reading and Language Skills Assessment

COMPREHENSION (continued)

Lisa and Emma were bored one day.

"What can we do to have fun?" Emma asked.

"I have an idea what you can do," Mom said. "Come to the kitchen with me."

Mom put some pudding mix and milk into a big bowl. She mixed it together to make pudding. Next, she put some of the pudding into three little bowls. Then, she added a different color food coloring to each bowl.

"I call this pudding paint," Mom said. "You can dip your fingers in the pudding and then use it to paint on paper."

"Thanks, Mom!" said Emma.

Lisa said, "I am going to paint a rabbit."

"I want to paint a horse and some flowers!" said Emma.

The girls ran to get some paper so they could get started.

31. What happens **right after** Mom says, "Come to the kitchen with me"?
- (A) Emma asks what they can do to have fun.
- (B) Mom puts pudding mix and milk into a bowl.
- (C) Mom adds food coloring to each bowl.
- (D) The girls run to get some paper.

32. Both Emma and Lisa decide to paint _____.
- (A) animals
- (B) rabbits
- (C) horses
- (D) flowers

GO ON ▶

Harcourt • Reading and Language Skills Assessment

COMPREHENSION (continued)

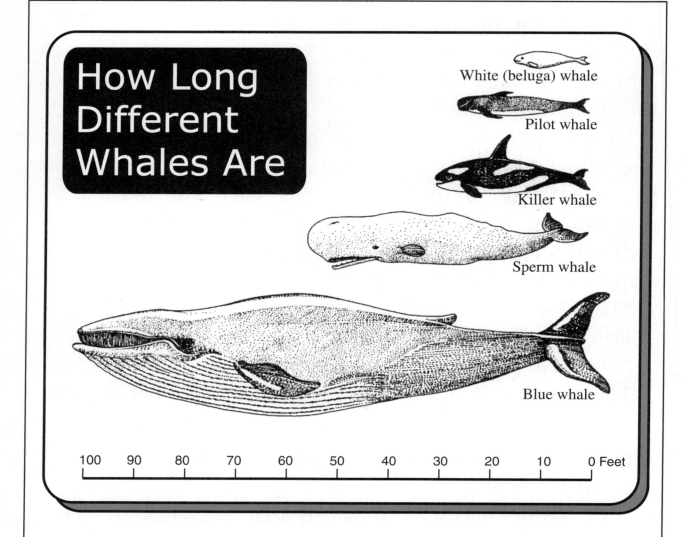

How Long Different Whales Are

White (beluga) whale

Pilot whale

Killer whale

Sperm whale

Blue whale

100 90 80 70 60 50 40 30 20 10 0 Feet

33. Which whale is the longest?
   Ⓐ White (beluga) whale
   Ⓑ Killer whale
   Ⓒ Sperm whale
   Ⓓ Blue whale

GO ON

Harcourt • Reading and Language Skills Assessment

COMPREHENSION (continued)

34. Which whale is about twice as long as the Killer whale?

Ⓐ White (beluga) whale

Ⓑ Pilot whale

Ⓒ Sperm whale

Ⓓ Blue whale

35. Which two whales are about the same size?

Ⓐ Pilot whale and Killer whale

Ⓑ White (beluga) whale and pilot whale

Ⓒ Sperm whale and Blue whale

Ⓓ White (beluga) whale and Sperm whale

36. Which whale is about half as long as the Killer whale?

Ⓐ Sperm whale

Ⓑ White (beluga) whale

Ⓒ Pilot whale

Ⓓ Blue whale

GO ON

COMPREHENSION (continued)

How to Make Cold Cereal

Here is a quick way to make breakfast. All you need is a box of cereal, milk, a bowl, and a spoon. First, get out a bowl and a spoon.

1. Open the box. Pour as much cereal as you want from the box into the bowl.

2. Add just enough milk for the cereal to float.

37. What do you do first?

Ⓐ add milk

Ⓑ pour the cereal

Ⓒ get out a bowl

Ⓓ open the box

GO ON ▶

COMPREHENSION (continued)

38. What is the spoon most likely used for?

Ⓐ to open the milk carton

Ⓑ to scoop the cereal

Ⓒ to add the milk

Ⓓ to eat the cereal

39. You should add enough milk to _____.

Ⓐ fill the bowl to the top

Ⓑ empty the milk carton

Ⓒ make the cereal float

Ⓓ fill a drinking glass

40. When are you most likely to use these directions?

Ⓐ breakfast

Ⓑ lunch

Ⓒ dinner

Ⓓ dessert

STOP

LANGUAGE

Sample

he can run fast

(A) he can run fast.

(B) He can run fast.

(C) correct as is

---

41. what a great show that was.

(A) what a great show that was?

(B) What a great show that was!

(C) correct as is

42. has the mail come yet!

(A) Has the mail come yet?

(B) has the mail come yet.

(C) correct as is

43. We have several <u>bunches</u> of grapes to eat.

(A) bunchs

(B) bunch

(C) correct as is

GO ON

LANGUAGE (continued)

44. Many <u>woman</u> were at the party.

Ⓐ womans

Ⓑ women

Ⓒ correct as is

45. I went to see <u>dr ben hays</u>.

Ⓐ Dr. Ben Hays

Ⓑ dr Ben Hays

Ⓓ correct as is

46. I have two pet fish named <u>Inky and Splash</u>.

Ⓐ inky and splash

Ⓑ inky and Splash

Ⓒ correct as is

47. I gave my teacher a card on <u>valentine's day</u>.

Ⓐ Valentine's Day

Ⓑ valentine's Day

Ⓒ correct as is

GO ON

LANGUAGE (continued)

48. We are leaving for our trip on <u>sunday, November 11</u>.

    (A) sunday, november 11

    (B) Sunday, November 11

    (C) correct as is

49. <u>The dog of my neighbor</u> is very friendly.

    (A) My neighbors dog

    (B) My neighbor dog's

    (C) My neighbor's dog

50. Can you see <u>the tail of the kite</u>?

    (A) the kite's tail

    (B) the kite tail's

    (C) the kites tail

STOP

Score_____

Harcourt • Reading and Language Skills Assessment

Just for You / Themes 1, 2, 3
Mid-Year Reading and Language Skills Assessment

Harcourt

Orlando   Boston   Dallas   Chicago   San Diego

Part No. 9997-37715-X

ISBN 0-15-332175-X (Package of 12)

2-1

TROPHIES

Reading and Language Skills Assessment Pretest

Banner Days / Theme 1

Name_____ Date_____

SKILL AREA	Criterion Score	Pupil Score	Pupil Strength
DECODING/PHONICS			
Vowel Dipthongs			
/ou/ou, ow	3/4	_____	_____
/oi/oi, oy	3/4	_____	_____
Vowel Digraphs			
/o͞o/oo, ue	3/4	_____	_____
Inflectional Endings			
-es (f to v)	3/4	_____	_____
Suffixes			
-ing, -ly, -ful, -less	3/4	_____	_____
VOCABULARY			
Antonyms	3/4	_____	_____
COMPREHENSION			
Cause and Effect	3/4	_____	_____
LANGUAGE	7/10	_____	_____
Pronouns			
Describing Words			
Words That Tell How Many			
Words That Compare			
TOTAL SCORE	28/38	_____	_____

Were accommodations made in administering this test? ☐ Yes ☐ No

Type of accommodations: _____

ISBN 0-15-332183-0

6 7 8 9 10   170   10 09 08 07 06 05 04

DECODING/PHONICS

<u>ou</u>t   <u>c</u>ow

Sample

Look at that _____ in the sky.

bird   joke   cloud   four
Ⓐ   Ⓑ   Ⓒ   Ⓓ

---

1. Do you hear that loud _____?

grow   gong   sound   sun
Ⓐ   Ⓑ   Ⓒ   Ⓓ

2. Come here right _____.

away   now   flow   long
Ⓐ   Ⓑ   Ⓒ   Ⓓ

3. We planted the seed in the _____.

ground   hole   cot   pour
Ⓐ   Ⓑ   Ⓒ   Ⓓ

4. Put the ball _____.

slow   down   there   bust
Ⓐ   Ⓑ   Ⓒ   Ⓓ

STOP

Harcourt • Reading and Language Skills Assessment

DECODING/PHONICS

<u>co</u>in   <u>oy</u>ster

Sample

May I play with your _____ truck?

try   new   toy   grow
Ⓐ   Ⓑ   Ⓒ   Ⓓ

---

5. I hope you _____ our play.

stir   enjoy   like   hose
Ⓐ   Ⓑ   Ⓒ   Ⓓ

6. It is so nice to hear your _____.

voice   lid   bone   song
Ⓐ   Ⓑ   Ⓒ   Ⓓ

7. It is not nice to _____ at other people.

buy   point   stare   top
Ⓐ   Ⓑ   Ⓒ   Ⓓ

8. Did you hear that loud _____?

long   sound   noise   sit
Ⓐ   Ⓑ   Ⓒ   Ⓓ

STOP

Harcourt • Reading and Language Skills Assessment

DECODING/PHONICS

soon   clue

Sample

The color I like best is _____.

green   look   tale   blue
Ⓐ   Ⓑ   Ⓒ   Ⓓ

---

9. May I go, _____?

big   book   too   please
Ⓐ   Ⓑ   Ⓒ   Ⓓ

10. When is Grandpa _____ to arrive?

due   tub   deck   going
Ⓐ   Ⓑ   Ⓒ   Ⓓ

11. I used _____ to stick the stars on the paper.

sled   drum   paste   glue
Ⓐ   Ⓑ   Ⓒ   Ⓓ

12. A story that really happened is _____.

beam   true   good   put
Ⓐ   Ⓑ   Ⓒ   Ⓓ

STOP

DECODING/PHONICS

Sample

They say that cats have nine _____.

life   lifes   lives   lifs
Ⓐ   Ⓑ   Ⓒ   Ⓓ

---

13. We bought two _____ of bread.

loafes   loaves   loaf   loafies
Ⓐ   Ⓑ   Ⓒ   Ⓓ

14. There are five _____ in the story.

elfies   elfes   elf   elves
Ⓐ   Ⓑ   Ⓒ   Ⓓ

15. That tree has lost all its _____.

leaves   leafes   leaf   leafs
Ⓐ   Ⓑ   Ⓒ   Ⓓ

16. Dad put six _____ in my room.

shelf   shelfes   shelves   shelfs
Ⓐ   Ⓑ   Ⓒ   Ⓓ

STOP

Score _____   *Banner Days* / Theme 1

DECODING/PHONICS

Sample

I am very _____ for your help.

thank   thanking   thankful   thankless

Ⓐ   Ⓑ   Ⓒ   Ⓓ

17. He walks very _____.

slowed   slowing   slowly   slows

Ⓐ   Ⓑ   Ⓒ   Ⓓ

18. You should be _____ to your teacher.

help   helpful   helps   helpless

Ⓐ   Ⓑ   Ⓒ   Ⓓ

19. I am tired because I had a _____ night.

sleepless   sleeps   sleep   sleeping

Ⓐ   Ⓑ   Ⓒ   Ⓓ

20. We are _____ a fun game!

playful   plays   play   playing

Ⓐ   Ⓑ   Ⓒ   Ⓓ

STOP

Harcourt • Reading and Language Skills Assessment

VOCABULARY: Antonyms

Sample

The opposite of <u>back</u> is _____ .

sun	dark	front	girl
Ⓐ	Ⓑ	Ⓒ	Ⓓ

---

21. The opposite of <u>always</u> is _____ .

far	never	early	over
Ⓐ	Ⓑ	Ⓒ	Ⓓ

22. The opposite of <u>strong</u> is _____ .

glad	good	weak	fast
Ⓐ	Ⓑ	Ⓒ	Ⓓ

23. The opposite of <u>before</u> is _____ .

long	inside	found	after
Ⓐ	Ⓑ	Ⓒ	Ⓓ

24. The opposite of <u>alone</u> is _____ .

together	mean	high	light
Ⓐ	Ⓑ	Ⓒ	Ⓓ

STOP

COMPREHENSION: Cause and Effect

> Sara was visiting her cousin Sam's farm. Everyone in Sam's family woke up early. It was still dark when Sara got dressed. "We have many jobs to do," Sam said to Sara. "You can help me carry hay to feed the horses." Sara saw Uncle Ned milking the cows.
>
> "We sell the milk," Sam said.
>
> When all the jobs were done, Sara was very hungry. She and Sam went back to the house for a big farm breakfast.

Sample

Why did everyone in Sam's family wake up early?

Ⓐ They were not tired.

Ⓑ They had many jobs to do.

Ⓒ They wanted lots of time to play.

Ⓓ Sara woke them up.

---

25. Why was it dark while Sara got dressed?

Ⓐ The sun had not come up yet.

Ⓑ The lights were not working.

Ⓒ It was late at night.

Ⓓ There were no lights in the old farm house.

GO ON ▶

COMPREHENSION: Cause and Effect (continued)

26. Why did Sara and Sam carry hay?

Ⓐ to build a fort

Ⓑ to clean out the barn

Ⓒ to feed the horses

Ⓓ to feed the cows

27. How does Sam's family make money?

Ⓐ They sell hay.

Ⓑ They sell milk.

Ⓒ They sell horses.

Ⓓ They work for other families.

28. Why was Sara so hungry?

Ⓐ She did not have lunch.

Ⓑ She gave her food to Sam.

Ⓒ She did not like to eat farm food.

Ⓓ She worked hard before breakfast.

STOP

Harcourt • Reading and Language Skills Assessment

LANGUAGE

Sample

Which word is a pronoun in this sentence?
She likes cookies.

Ⓐ She

Ⓑ likes

Ⓒ cookies

29. Which word is a pronoun in this sentence?

Did you watch the game?

Ⓐ Did

Ⓑ you

Ⓒ watch

30. Which is the best pronoun for the underlined word?

Jim painted a picture of a fish.

Ⓐ They

Ⓑ It

Ⓒ He

GO ON ▶

LANGUAGE (continued)

31. Which is the best pronoun for the underlined words?

The frogs hopped in the pond.

Ⓐ They

Ⓑ You

Ⓒ He

32. Which is the describing word in this sentence?

We saw some white clouds.

Ⓐ We

Ⓑ saw

Ⓒ white

33. Which is the describing word in this sentence?

The kitten has soft fur.

Ⓐ kitten

Ⓑ soft

Ⓒ fur

34. Which describing word tells how many in this sentence?

She put two eggs in a bowl.

Ⓐ put

Ⓑ two

Ⓒ eggs

GO ON ▶

LANGUAGE (continued)

35. Which describing word tells how many in
this sentence?

We saw some monkeys at the zoo.

Ⓐ some

Ⓑ monkeys

Ⓒ zoo

36. Which word in this sentence is a word that compares?

This pup is the smallest in the litter.

Ⓐ pup

Ⓑ smallest

Ⓒ litter

37. Which word best completes this sentence?

He is the _____ of all the boys in the race.

Ⓐ fast

Ⓑ faster

Ⓒ fastest

38. Which word best completes this sentence?

I am _____ than you are.

Ⓐ old

Ⓑ older

Ⓒ oldest

STOP

Imagine That! / Theme 1

Reading and Language Skills Assessment

Harcourt

Orlando   Boston   Dallas   Chicago   San Diego

Part No. 9997-37720-6

ISBN 0-15-332183-0 (Package of 12)

2-2

TROPHIES

Reading and Language Skills Assessment Posttest

Banner Days / Theme 1

Name_____ Date_____

SKILL AREA	Criterion Score	Pupil Score	Pupil Strength
DECODING/PHONICS			
Vowel Dipthongs			
/ou/ou, ow	3/4	_____	_____
/oi/oi, oy	3/4	_____	_____
Vowel Digraphs			
/o͞o/oo, ue	3/4	_____	_____
Inflectional Endings			
-es (f to v)	3/4	_____	_____
Suffixes			
-ing, -ly, -ful, -less	3/4	_____	_____
VOCABULARY			
Antonyms	3/4	_____	_____
COMPREHENSION			
Cause and Effect	3/4	_____	_____
LANGUAGE	7/10	_____	_____
Pronouns			
Describing Words			
Words That Tell How Many			
Words That Compare			
TOTAL SCORE	28/38	_____	_____

Were accommodations made in administering this test? ❏ Yes ❏ No

Type of accommodations: _____

Printed in the United States of America

ISBN 0-15-332183-0

6 7 8 9 10   170   10 09 08 07 06 05 04

DECODING/PHONICS

<u>**out**</u>   <u>**cow**</u>

Sample

Look at that _____ in the sky.

bird   joke   cloud   four
Ⓐ   Ⓑ   Ⓒ   Ⓓ

---

1. We ran _____ the house.

course   shut   around   inside
Ⓐ   Ⓑ   Ⓒ   Ⓓ

2. The king had on a gold _____.

ring   crown   boat   dose
Ⓐ   Ⓑ   Ⓒ   Ⓓ

3. Don't _____ on the table.

pound   draw   plump   drone
Ⓐ   Ⓑ   Ⓒ   Ⓓ

4. I like the color _____.

brown   bunk   blue   lock
Ⓐ   Ⓑ   Ⓒ   Ⓓ

STOP

Harcourt • Reading and Language Skills Assessment

DECODING/PHONICS

co<u>i</u>n   <u>oy</u>ster

Sample

May I play with your _____ truck?

try   new   toy   grow
Ⓐ   Ⓑ   Ⓒ   Ⓓ

---

5. May I _____ your new club?

cone   job   join   visit
Ⓐ   Ⓑ   Ⓒ   Ⓓ

6. He is such a good _____.

child   boy   nose   thin
Ⓐ   Ⓑ   Ⓒ   Ⓓ

7. Dad put some _____ in the car.

shout   shrub   gas   oil
Ⓐ   Ⓑ   Ⓒ   Ⓓ

8. The pot of water has started to _____.

boil   bone   steam   tie
Ⓐ   Ⓑ   Ⓒ   Ⓓ

STOP

Harcourt • Reading and Language Skills Assessment

DECODING/PHONICS

<u>soo</u>n   cl<u>ue</u>

Sample

The color I like best is _____.

green   look   tale   blue
Ⓐ   Ⓑ   Ⓒ   Ⓓ

---

9. We saw many animals at the _____.

took   farm   three   zoo
Ⓐ   Ⓑ   Ⓒ   Ⓓ

10. Give me a _____ to help me solve the puzzle.

chill   clue   but   hint
Ⓐ   Ⓑ   Ⓒ   Ⓓ

11. My best friend is named _____.

Sue   Fred   Bud   Tom
Ⓐ   Ⓑ   Ⓒ   Ⓓ

12. We ate _____ muffins for breakfast.

plum   apple   blueberry send
Ⓐ   Ⓑ   Ⓒ   Ⓓ

STOP

DECODING/PHONICS

Sample

They say that cats have nine _____.

life	lifes	lives	lifs
Ⓐ	Ⓑ	Ⓒ	Ⓓ

---

13. There are two new _____ in the barn.

calf	calfies	calves	calfes
Ⓐ	Ⓑ	Ⓒ	Ⓓ

14. Three _____ sneaked into the house.

thieves	thief	thiefes	thiefs
Ⓐ	Ⓑ	Ⓒ	Ⓓ

15. Please put four forks, spoons, and _____ on the table.

knife	knifes	knifies	knives
Ⓐ	Ⓑ	Ⓒ	Ⓓ

16. All ten _____ followed their leader.

wolf	wolves	wolfs	wolfes
Ⓐ	Ⓑ	Ⓒ	Ⓓ

STOP

Score _____ *Banner Days / Theme 1*

Harcourt • Reading and Language Skills Assessment

DECODING/PHONICS

Sample

I am very _____ for your help.

thank	thanking	thankful	thankless
Ⓐ	Ⓑ	Ⓒ	Ⓓ

---

17. If you answer the questions _____, you will make a good grade.

corrects	correcting	correctly	corrected
Ⓐ	Ⓑ	Ⓒ	Ⓓ

18. I am so happy and _____ today!

joys	joyless	joy	joyful
Ⓐ	Ⓑ	Ⓒ	Ⓓ

19. That man is very strong, brave, and _____.

fearless	fears	fearing	fearful
Ⓐ	Ⓑ	Ⓒ	Ⓓ

20. Doing a lot of hard work is very_____.

tires	tiring	tire	tireless
Ⓐ	Ⓑ	Ⓒ	Ⓓ

STOP

Harcourt • Reading and Language Skills Assessment

VOCABULARY: Antonyms

Sample

The opposite of <u>back</u> is _____ .

sun
Ⓐ

dark
Ⓑ

front
Ⓒ

girl
Ⓓ

---

21. The opposite of <u>new</u> is _____ .

near
Ⓐ

fun
Ⓑ

little
Ⓒ

old
Ⓓ

22. The opposite of <u>easy</u> is _____ .

sad
Ⓐ

big
Ⓑ

hard
Ⓒ

slow
Ⓓ

23. The opposite of <u>begin</u> is _____ .

short
Ⓐ

end
Ⓑ

lost
Ⓒ

stay
Ⓓ

24. The opposite of <u>quiet</u> is _____ .

loud
Ⓐ

sweet
Ⓑ

up
Ⓒ

dark
Ⓓ

STOP

Harcourt • Reading and Language Skills Assessment

COMPREHENSION: Cause and Effect

It was a hot summer. Joey was bored with playing quietly inside. He felt like running and jumping and making noise. He wanted to play *outside*. His sister, Karen, said it was too hot to go outside.

Then Joey had an idea. He went to ask Mom something. Mom nodded her head to say yes. Then Joey put on his swimsuit. He went out in the yard. He got the garden hose and turned on the water. He pointed the hose up in the air. The water came down like rain. Joey jumped around under the cool water.

Karen looked out the window and saw Joey playing in the water. She ran to put on her swimsuit, too. Then she hurried outside. Joey had found a good way to have fun outside on a hot day.

Sample

Joey wanted to go outside because he was _____.

Ⓐ noisy

Ⓑ sad

Ⓒ bored

Ⓓ tired

GO ON

COMPREHENSION: Cause and Effect (continued)

25. At first, why didn't Karen want to go outside?

(A) It was raining.

(B) It was too hot.

(C) She was too busy.

(D) She was helping Mom.

26. What happened when Joey got an idea?

(A) He started to run and jump.

(B) He played quietly inside.

(C) He put on his swimsuit.

(D) He told Karen about it.

27. Joey pointed the hose up into the air because he wanted to _____.

(A) splash some birds

(B) play in the cool water

(C) wash the windows

(D) water the garden

28. Why did Karen hurry outside?

(A) She thought that it was raining.

(B) It was time to go to swim lessons.

(C) It was too hot in the house.

(D) She wanted to play in the water, too.

STOP

Score _____

Harcourt • Reading and Language Skills Assessment

LANGUAGE

Sample

Which word is a pronoun in this sentence?
She likes cookies.

(A) She

(B) likes

(C) cookies

29. Which word is a pronoun in this sentence?

May I have a plum?

(A) May

(B) I

(C) plum

30. Which is the best pronoun for the underlined word?

Ann skated across the ice.

(A) She

(B) It

(C) They

31. Which is the best pronoun for the underlined words?

The ducks are walking by the lake.

(A) She

(B) It

(C) They

GO ON

LANGUAGE (continued)

32. Which is the describing word in this sentence?

A boat sailed in the blue water.

Ⓐ boat

Ⓑ sailed

Ⓒ blue

33. Which is the describing word in this sentence?

She tripped on the slick ice.

Ⓐ tripped

Ⓑ slick

Ⓒ ice

34. Which describing word tells how many in this sentence?

There are six fish in the bowl.

Ⓐ six

Ⓑ fish

Ⓒ bowl

35. Which describing word tells how many in this sentence?

Farmer Dan has many pigs on his farm.

Ⓐ has

Ⓑ many

Ⓒ farm

GO ON ▶

Harcourt • Reading and Language Skills Assessment

LANGUAGE (continued)

36. Which word in this sentence is a word that compares?

It is colder today than yesterday.

Ⓐ It

Ⓑ is

Ⓒ colder

37. Which word best completes this sentence?

This building is _____ than that one.

Ⓐ tall

Ⓑ taller

Ⓒ tallest

38. Which word best completes this sentence?

That frog croaked the _____ of all the frogs in the pond.

Ⓐ loud

Ⓑ louder

Ⓒ loudest

STOP

Imagine That! / Theme 1
Reading and Language Skills Assessment

Harcourt

Orlando   Boston   Dallas   Chicago   San Diego

Part No. 9997-37717-6

ISBN 0-15-332183-0 (Package of 12)

2-2

TROPHIES

Reading and Language Skills Assessment Pretest

Banner Days / Theme 2

Name _____ Date _____

SKILL AREA	Criterion Score	Pupil Score	Pupil Strength
DECODING/PHONICS			
Vowel Digraphs /oo/ew, ui	3/4	_____	_____
Contractions 'll, n't, 's	3/4	_____	_____
Prefixes re-, pre-, mis-, under-	3/4	_____	_____
Suffixes -er, -est	3/4	_____	_____
VOCABULARY			
Multiple-Meaning Words	3/4	_____	_____
COMPREHENSION			
Summarize/Restate Information	3/4	_____	_____
LITERARY RESPONSE AND ANALYSIS			
Narrative Elements (Plot, Setting, Character)	3/4	_____	_____
LANGUAGE	7/10	_____	_____
Verbs That Tell About Now			
Agreement			
Past-Tense Verbs			
Am, Is, Are, Was, Were			
Has, Have, Had			
TOTAL SCORE	28/38	_____	_____

Were accommodations made in administering this test? ☐ Yes ☐ No

Type of accommodations: _____

ISBN 0-15-332183-0

6 7 8 9 10   170   10 09 08 07 06 05 04

DECODING/PHONICS

grew   bruise

Sample

What kind of _____ do you like to eat?

hut   fruit   never   cake
Ⓐ   Ⓑ   Ⓒ   Ⓓ

---

1. Would you like some _____ to drink?

mule   milk   price   juice
Ⓐ   Ⓑ   Ⓒ   Ⓓ

2. We watched a cow _____ its food.

chew   dust   eat   met
Ⓐ   Ⓑ   Ⓒ   Ⓓ

3. Mom is cooking _____ for supper.

crib   stew   beef   blush
Ⓐ   Ⓑ   Ⓒ   Ⓓ

4. Dad has on a black _____.

whine   tug   suit   tie
Ⓐ   Ⓑ   Ⓒ   Ⓓ

STOP

Harcourt • Reading and Language Skills Assessment

DECODING/PHONICS

Sample

I <u>do not</u> have the key.

didn't	don't	can't	won't
Ⓐ	Ⓑ	Ⓒ	Ⓓ

5. <u>He is</u> my teacher.

What's	She's	It's	He's
Ⓐ	Ⓑ	Ⓒ	Ⓓ

6. <u>They will</u> help us.

You'll	They'll	I'll	We'll
Ⓐ	Ⓑ	Ⓒ	Ⓓ

7. I <u>cannot</u> reach it.

isn't	doesn't	can't	haven't
Ⓐ	Ⓑ	Ⓒ	Ⓓ

8. <u>It is</u> my birthday.

It's	Who's	There's	Here's
Ⓐ	Ⓑ	Ⓒ	Ⓓ

STOP

Harcourt • Reading and Language Skills Assessment

DECODING/PHONICS

Sample

    The little mole has a home deep _____.

    grounded   underground   reground   grounding

    Ⓐ   Ⓑ   Ⓒ   Ⓓ

9. We will _____ the stove so it will be hot when we put the cake in to bake.

    preheat   underheat   heats   heating

    Ⓐ   Ⓑ   Ⓒ   Ⓓ

10. I lost my homework, so I had to _____ it all.

    did   redo   doing   misdo

    Ⓐ   Ⓑ   Ⓒ   Ⓓ

11. Did you _____ him for someone else?

    mistake   takes   taking   retake

    Ⓐ   Ⓑ   Ⓒ   Ⓓ

12. That worker did a good job, so do not _____ him.

    paying   prepay   underpay   pays

    Ⓐ   Ⓑ   Ⓒ   Ⓓ

STOP

DECODING/PHONICS

Sample

I am the _____ of the three children in our family.

old   older   oldest   olds
Ⓐ   Ⓑ   Ⓒ   Ⓓ

---

13. This loaf of bread is _____ than that one.

fresh   fresher   freshest   freshing
Ⓐ   Ⓑ   Ⓒ   Ⓓ

14. That is the _____ building in town.

tall   taller   tallest   talls
Ⓐ   Ⓑ   Ⓒ   Ⓓ

15. That pup is the _____ of all.

small   smaller   smallest   smalls
Ⓐ   Ⓑ   Ⓒ   Ⓓ

16. This door is _____ than that door.

wide   wider   widest   wides
Ⓐ   Ⓑ   Ⓒ   Ⓓ

STOP

Harcourt • Reading and Language Skills Assessment

VOCABULARY: Multiple-Meaning Words

Sample

Read this sentence.

Mom used a needle and thread to do some sewing.

What does the word *needle* mean in this sentence?

(A) to tease someone

(B) a sharp tool used for stitching

(C) a pointer on a compass

(D) a thin leaf on a tree

17. Read this sentence.

I will hit the ball out of the ball park.

What does the word *hit* mean in this sentence?

(A) to strike something

(B) to think of an idea

(C) a song on the radio

(D) to get along well

18. Read this sentence.

I can carry the box because it is light.

What does the word *light* mean in this sentence?

(A) to land on a branch

(B) to make a candle burn

(C) not very heavy

(D) sunny and bright

GO ON

VOCABULARY: Multiple-Meaning Words (continued)

19. Read this sentence.

My <u>back</u> is stiff and sore.

In which sentence does the word <u>back</u> mean the same thing as in the sentence above?

Ⓐ Give <u>back</u> my pencil, please.

Ⓑ Will you rub my <u>back</u>?

Ⓒ Get in the <u>back</u> of the car.

Ⓓ <u>Back</u> away from the fire.

20. Read this sentence.

The game is <u>over</u>.

In which sentence does the word <u>over</u> mean the same thing as in the sentence above?

Ⓐ When the show is <u>over</u>, I will help you.

Ⓑ My uncle is staying <u>over</u> the holidays.

Ⓒ Can you get <u>over</u> the high fence?

Ⓓ Hang the picture <u>over</u> the door.

STOP

COMPREHENSION: Summarize/Restate Information

Digger the Dog woke up from a deep sleep. He got up and began to dig a hole. Before long, he had dug up a bone! He chewed on the bone, but he wanted more to eat. Soon his owner, Kim, came and gave Digger some dog food.

Sample

Which is the best summary of this story?

(A) Digger the Dog woke up from a deep sleep.

(B) Digger the Dog got up and began to dig a hole.

(C) Digger the Dog woke up, dug up a bone, chewed on the bone, and soon got some dog food from his owner.

(D) Digger the Dog chewed on a bone, but he wanted more to eat.

Harcourt • Reading and Language Skills Assessment

GO ON

COMPREHENSION: Summarize/Restate Information (continued)

Each ant in an ant hill has work to do. Some of the ants dig little rooms in the ant hill. Some ants bring food for all the ants to eat. Other ants store the food to save it for another time.

21. Which is the best summary of this story?

Ⓐ Some of the ants dig little rooms in the ant hill.

Ⓑ Other ants store the food to save it for another time.

Ⓒ Each ant in an ant hill has work to do, such as digging rooms, bringing food, or storing food.

Ⓓ Some ants bring food for all the ants to eat.

GO ON

COMPREHENSION: Summarize/Restate Information (continued)

A dog really is man's best friend. A dog never says mean things to you. A dog always acts happy to see you when you come home. A dog will always stay by your side even when you are no fun to be around.

22. Which is the best summary of this story?

Ⓐ A dog never says mean things to you.

Ⓑ A dog will always stay by your side even when you are no fun to be around.

Ⓒ A dog always acts happy to see you when you come home.

Ⓓ A dog really is man's best friend because it never says mean things, acts happy to see you, and will always stay by your side.

GO ON

COMPREHENSION: Summarize/Restate Information (continued)

Raul went to a fair with his family. He rode the fast rides and ate pink cotton candy. Then he went to a big tank full of water and fish. A man there showed Raul how to throw a fishing line in the water. Raul felt a tug on the line. He had caught a fish!

23. Which is the best summary of this story?

Ⓐ Raul rode the fast rides and ate pink cotton candy.

Ⓑ Raul went to a fair, rode the rides, ate cotton candy, and caught a fish.

Ⓒ Raul went to a big tank full of water and fish.

Ⓓ Raul felt a tug on the line.

GO ON

COMPREHENSION: Summarize/Restate Information (continued)

Tina's aunt took her to a powwow. It was a special dance for Indian people. Tina saw girls in bright dresses. Some of the dresses had little silver bells. "Those are called jingle dresses," her aunt said. Tina watched the girls dance. She wished that she had a jingle dress.

24. Which is the best summary of this story?

Ⓐ Tina's aunt took her to a powwow, a special dance for Indian people.

Ⓑ Tina went to a powwow, watched girls dancing, and wished that she had a jingle dress.

Ⓒ Some of the dresses had little silver bells.

Ⓓ Tina saw girls in bright dresses.

STOP

LITERARY RESPONSE AND ANALYSIS: Narrative Elements

Max and Nan were friends. They played together every afternoon. They played ball. They played tag. They got along very well—just the two of them.

One day Max and Nan were playing outside. They saw a little boy watching them. They wished he would go away.

"Who are you?" asked Nan. "What are you doing here?"

"My name is Ben," the boy said. "My family just moved in next door."

Max looked at Nan. Nan looked at Max. Then they both smiled.

"Would you like to play ball with us?" Max asked.

After that, Max and Nan and Ben were friends. They got along very well—just the three of them.

25. Who is this story mostly about?

   Ⓐ Ben

   Ⓑ Max and Nan

   Ⓒ a new family next door

   Ⓓ Nan's friends at school

GO ON

LITERARY RESPONSE AND ANALYSIS: Narrative Elements (continued)

26. Where were the children playing?

    Ⓐ in Nan's house

    Ⓑ at school

    Ⓒ outside

    Ⓓ in Ben's house

27. When did this story take place?

    Ⓐ before breakfast

    Ⓑ in the afternoon

    Ⓒ at supper time

    Ⓓ at bed time

28. What happens at the end of the story?

    Ⓐ The children become friends.

    Ⓑ Ben's family moves away.

    Ⓒ Max tells Ben to leave.

    Ⓓ Nan plays inside.

STOP

Harcourt • Reading and Language Skills Assessment

LANGUAGE

Sample

Which word is the verb in this sentence?
The kitten licked its paws.

(A) kitten

(B) licked

(C) paws

---

29. Which word is the verb in this sentence?
The moon shines in the sky.

(A) moon

(B) shines

(C) sky

30. Which verb best completes this sentence?
The dog _____ the ball.

(A) fetch

(B) fetchs

(C) fetches

31. Which verb best completes this sentence?
Two friends _____ down the road.

(A) walk

(B) walkes

(C) walks

GO ON ▶

Harcourt • Reading and Language Skills Assessment

LANGUAGE (continued)

32. Which verb best completes this sentence?

He _____ the bike tire.

(A) fixs

(B) fixes

(C) fix

33. Which is the verb that tells about the past in this sentence?

Last week I visited my friend.

(A) Last

(B) week

(C) visited

34. Which verb tells about the past to complete this sentence?

Yesterday I _____ my plant.

(A) water

(B) watered

(C) waters

GO ON

LANGUAGE (continued)

35. Which verb best completes this sentence?
These strawberries _____ good.

Ⓐ am

Ⓑ is

Ⓒ are

36. Which verb best completes this sentence?
The baby seal _____ sleeping.

Ⓐ was

Ⓑ were

Ⓒ be

37. Which verb best completes this sentence?
Giraffes _____ long necks.

Ⓐ has

Ⓑ have

Ⓒ had

38. Which verb best completes this sentence?
Yesterday Anna _____ a cold.

Ⓐ has

Ⓑ have

Ⓒ had

STOP

Score _____   *Banner Days / Theme 2*

· T R O P H I E S ·

Neighborhood News / Theme 2
Reading and Language Skills Assessment

Harcourt

Orlando   Boston   Dallas   Chicago   San Diego

Part No. 9997-37721-4

ISBN 0-15-332183-0 (Package of 12)

2-2

· T R O P H I E S ·

Reading and Language Skills Assessment Posttest

Banner Days / Theme 2

Name _____ Date _____

SKILL AREA	Criterion Score	Pupil Score	Pupil Strength
DECODING/PHONICS			
Vowel Digraphs /$\overline{oo}$/ew, ui	3/4	_____	_____
Contractions 'll, n't, 's	3/4	_____	_____
Prefixes re-, pre-, mis-, under-	3/4	_____	_____
Suffixes -er, -est	3/4	_____	_____
VOCABULARY			
Multiple-Meaning Words	3/4	_____	_____
COMPREHENSION			
Summarize/Restate Information	3/4	_____	_____
LITERARY RESPONSE AND ANALYSIS			
Narrative Elements (Plot, Setting, Character)	3/4	_____	_____
LANGUAGE	7/10		
Verbs That Tell About Now			
Agreement			
Past-Tense Verbs			
Am, Is, Are, Was, Were			
Has, Have, Had			
TOTAL SCORE	28/38	_____	_____

Were accommodations made in administering this test?   ☐ Yes   ☐ No

Type of accommodations: _____

Printed in the United States of America

ISBN 0-15-332183-0

6 7 8 9 10   170   10 09 08 07 06 05 04

DECODING/PHONICS

gr<u>ew</u>   **br<u>ui</u>se**

Sample

What kind of _____ do you like to eat?

hut	fruit	never	cake
Ⓐ	Ⓑ	Ⓒ	Ⓓ

---

1. I _____ the answer to the question.

knew	grill	meet	had
Ⓐ	Ⓑ	Ⓒ	Ⓓ

2. They went on a river _____.

sell	cruise	lid	ride
Ⓐ	Ⓑ	Ⓒ	Ⓓ

3. Tim _____ the ball to Emmy.

kind	gave	greet	threw
Ⓐ	Ⓑ	Ⓒ	Ⓓ

4. How did you _____ your arm?

tin	bruise	hurt	greet
Ⓐ	Ⓑ	Ⓒ	Ⓓ

STOP

Harcourt • Reading and Language Skills Assessment

DECODING/PHONICS

Sample

   I <u>do not</u> have the key.

didn't	don't	can't	won't
Ⓐ	Ⓑ	Ⓒ	Ⓓ

---

5. <u>We will</u> go with you.

You'll	She'll	We'll	He'll
Ⓐ	Ⓑ	Ⓒ	Ⓓ

6. <u>That is</u> my kitten.

It's	That's	She's	Here's
Ⓐ	Ⓑ	Ⓒ	Ⓓ

7. That <u>was not</u> what I said.

wasn't	aren't	couldn't	shouldn't
Ⓐ	Ⓑ	Ⓒ	Ⓓ

8. She <u>has not</u> come home yet.

didn't	won't	hasn't	isn't
Ⓐ	Ⓑ	Ⓒ	Ⓓ

STOP

Harcourt • Reading and Language Skills Assessment

DECODING/PHONICS

Sample

The little mole has a home deep _____.

grounded	underground	reground	grounding
Ⓐ	Ⓑ	Ⓒ	Ⓓ

9. We will _____ the food so it will be ready to eat later.

cooks	precook	cooked	undercook
Ⓐ	Ⓑ	Ⓒ	Ⓓ

10. Do you _____ where we have seen that man before?

miscall	calling	calls	recall
Ⓐ	Ⓑ	Ⓒ	Ⓓ

11. The newspaper has a _____ in it, so they will have to fix it.

misprint	prints	printed	reprint
Ⓐ	Ⓑ	Ⓒ	Ⓓ

12. Do not _____ a job that you cannot finish.

takes	taking	undertake	retake
Ⓐ	Ⓑ	Ⓒ	Ⓓ

STOP

DECODING/PHONICS

Sample

I am the _____ of the three children in our family.

old
Ⓐ

older
Ⓑ

oldest
Ⓒ

olds
Ⓓ

---

13. I can run _____ than you can.

fast
Ⓐ

faster
Ⓑ

fastest
Ⓒ

fasts
Ⓓ

14. My room is the _____ room in the house.

clean
Ⓐ

cleaner
Ⓑ

cleanest
Ⓒ

cleans
Ⓓ

15. This nail is _____ than that one.

long
Ⓐ

longer
Ⓑ

longest
Ⓒ

longing
Ⓓ

16. This cake tastes the _____ of the three cakes.

sweet
Ⓐ

sweeter
Ⓑ

sweetest
Ⓒ

sweets
Ⓓ

STOP

Score _____

Harcourt • Reading and Language Skills Assessment

VOCABULARY: Multiple-Meaning Words

Sample

Read this sentence.

Mom used a needle and thread to do some sewing.

What does the word *needle* mean in this sentence?

Ⓐ to tease someone

Ⓑ a sharp tool used for stitching

Ⓒ a pointer on a compass

Ⓓ a thin leaf on a tree

17. Read this sentence.

This car runs well.

What does the word *runs* mean in this sentence?

Ⓐ tears in a stocking

Ⓑ works smoothly

Ⓒ is in a race

Ⓓ baseball scores

18. Read this sentence.

Did you put a stamp on your letter?

What does the word *stamp* mean in this sentence?

Ⓐ to walk with heavy steps

Ⓑ a picture printed on cloth

Ⓒ a small sticker put on mail

Ⓓ to put out a fire

GO ON

VOCABULARY: Multiple-Meaning Words (continued)

19. Read this sentence.

She has a gold ring on her finger.

In which sentence does the word ring mean the same thing as in the sentence above?

Ⓐ Please ring the bell.

Ⓑ There are lions in the circus ring.

Ⓒ I have a ruby ring on my right hand.

Ⓓ The crowd made a ring around the speaker.

20. Read this sentence.

The sign tells how much things cost.

In which sentence does the word sign mean the same thing as in the sentence above?

Ⓐ The sign tells what time the store opens.

Ⓑ Dad will sign his name on the check.

Ⓒ Are you going to sign up for the race?

Ⓓ A fever is a sign that you are sick.

STOP

Score _____

Harcourt • Reading and Language Skills Assessment

COMPREHENSION: Summarize/Restate Information

Digger the Dog woke up from a deep sleep. He got up and began to dig a hole. Before long, he had dug up a bone! He chewed on the bone, but he wanted more to eat. Soon his owner, Kim, came and gave Digger some dog food.

Sample

Which is the best summary of this story?

A Digger the Dog woke up from a deep sleep.

B Digger the Dog got up and began to dig a hole.

C Digger the Dog woke up, dug up a bone, chewed on the bone, and soon got some dog food from his owner.

D Digger the Dog chewed on a bone, but he wanted more to eat.

GO ON

COMPREHENSION: Summarize/Restate Information (continued)

Sam and Jen went to the park. First, they watched some ducks swim in the lake. Next, Sam and Jen went for a long walk. After their walk, the children sat on a blanket and ate a basket lunch.

21. Which is the best summary of this story?

Ⓐ First, Sam and Jen watched some ducks swim in the lake.

Ⓑ Sam and Jen went to the park, watched ducks swim, went for a walk, and then ate a basket lunch.

Ⓒ Next, Sam and Jen went for a long walk.

Ⓓ After their walk, the children sat on a blanket and ate a basket lunch.

GO ON

COMPREHENSION: Summarize/Restate Information (continued)

There are many people who work each day to help you. Doctors are ready to help you get well if you get sick. Firefighters stand by in case they are needed to put out a fire. There are even people who make sure you have clean water to drink.

22. Which is the best summary of this story?

Ⓐ Doctors are ready to help you get well if you get sick.

Ⓑ Many people work each day to help you, such as doctors, firefighters, and people who make sure you have clean water.

Ⓒ There are even people who make sure you have clean water to drink.

Ⓓ Firefighters stand by in case they are needed to put out a fire.

GO ON

COMPREHENSION: Summarize/Restate Information (continued)

> Ken has a dog named Sweetie. He takes good care of his dog. He feeds her and gives her fresh water every day. He brushes her soft fur to keep it clean and shiny. He plays with Sweetie every day. If Sweetie gets sick, Ken takes her to the doctor.

23. Which is the best summary of this story?

Ⓐ Ken has a dog named Sweetie.

Ⓑ He brushes her soft fur to keep it clean and shiny.

Ⓒ Ken takes care of his dog, Sweetie, by feeding her, brushing her, playing with her, and taking her to the doctor.

Ⓓ Ken plays with Sweetie every day.

GO ON

COMPREHENSION: Summarize/Restate Information (continued)

Ann decided to have a costume parade. She invited all the children on her street. She told everyone to meet at five o'clock on Saturday.

When Saturday came, the children put on their costumes. Then they walked down the sidewalk to the park. At the park, Ann's parents served cake and ice cream.

24. Which is the best summary of this story?

Ⓐ When Ann planned a costume parade, the children wore costumes, walked to the park, and had cake and ice cream.

Ⓑ Ann invited all the children on her street.

Ⓒ She told everyone to meet at five o'clock on Saturday.

Ⓓ They walked down the sidewalk to the park.

STOP

LITERARY RESPONSE AND ANALYSIS: Narrative Elements

A fire truck raced down the street! It stopped at Jack's house. Two firefighters jumped out of the truck and ran to the front door. Jack's mother opened the door. Then she took them to her backyard. "Look up there! It's Trixie!" she cried.

The firefighters looked up. High in the tree was a little kitten. The kitten had climbed up too high, and it could not get down.

The firefighters put a ladder next to the tree. In a few minutes, Trixie was safe in the house, drinking milk from a bowl.

25. Where did this story take place?

Ⓐ on a fire truck

Ⓑ on a farm

Ⓒ in Jack's backyard

Ⓓ at Jack's school

26. Who is Trixie in this story?

Ⓐ a firefighter

Ⓑ Jack's mother

Ⓒ Jack's friend

Ⓓ a kitten

GO ON

LITERARY RESPONSE AND ANALYSIS: Narrative Elements (continued)

27. What did the firefighters do at Jack's house?

Ⓐ put out a fire

Ⓑ played a game

Ⓒ helped a kitten

Ⓓ took Jack's mother to a doctor

28. At the end of the story, Jack's mother must have felt_____.

Ⓐ afraid

Ⓑ happy

Ⓒ brave

Ⓓ worried

STOP

Harcourt • Reading and Language Skills Assessment

LANGUAGE

Sample

Which word is the verb in this sentence?
The kitten licked its paws.

(A) kitten

(B) licked

(C) paws

---

29. Which word is the verb in this sentence?
The stars twinkle at night.

(A) stars

(B) twinkle

(C) night

30. Which verb best completes this sentence?
She _____ the torn dress.

(A) patch

(B) patches

(C) patchs

31. Which verb best completes this sentence?
Three children _____ library books.

(A) read

(B) reades

(C) reads

GO ON

LANGUAGE (continued)

32. Which verb best completes this sentence?

He _____ the cake batter.

(A) mixs

(B) mixes

(C) mix

33. Which is the verb that tells about the past in this sentence?

Last week she moved to a new house.

(A) week

(B) she

(C) moved

34. Which verb tells about the past to complete this sentence?

Yesterday I _____ the car.

(A) wash

(B) washed

(C) washes

GO ON

LANGUAGE (continued)

35. Which verb best completes this sentence?
The brownies _____ great!

Ⓐ am

Ⓑ is

Ⓒ are

36. Which verb best completes this sentence?
The little pup _____ barking.

Ⓐ was

Ⓑ were

Ⓒ be

37. Which verb best completes this sentence?
An elephant _____ a long trunk.

Ⓐ has

Ⓑ have

Ⓒ had

38. Which verb best completes this sentence?
Yesterday you _____ a different lunch.

Ⓐ has

Ⓑ have

Ⓒ had

STOP

Score _____   *Banner Days / Theme 2*

Harcourt • Reading and Language Skills Assessment

Neighborhood News / Theme 2
Reading and Language Skills Assessment

Harcourt

Orlando   Boston   Dallas   Chicago   San Diego

Part No. 9997-37718-4

ISBN 0-15-332183-0 (Package of 12)

2-2

TROPHIES

Reading and Language Skills Assessment Pretest

Banner Days / Theme 3

Name_____ Date_____

SKILL AREA	Criterion Score	Pupil Score	Pupil Strength
DECODING/PHONICS			
R-controlled Vowels			
/âr/*air, are*	3/4	_____	_____
Vowel Variants			
/o͞o/*oo, ou*	3/4	_____	_____
/ô/*aw, au(gh)*	3/4	_____	_____
Vowel Digraphs			
/o͞o/*ou, ou(gh)*	3/4	_____	_____
Prefixes			
over-, un-	3/4	_____	_____
VOCABULARY			
Homophones	3/4	_____	_____
COMPREHENSION			
Locate Information: Book Parts	4/6	_____	_____
LANGUAGE	7/10	_____	_____
See, Give, Saw, Gave			
Come, Run, Came, Ran			
Go, Do, Went, Did			
Helping Verbs			
TOTAL SCORE	29/40	_____	_____

Were accommodations made in administering this test? ☐ Yes ☐ No

Type of accommodations: _____

_____

ISBN 0-15-332183-0

6 7 8 9 10   170   10 09 08 07 06 05 04

DECODING/PHONICS

chair   **bare**

Sample

Will you _____ your toys?

mad	star	share	bring
Ⓐ	Ⓑ	Ⓒ	Ⓓ

1. The kite went up high in the _____.

bran	air	bar	sky
Ⓐ	Ⓑ	Ⓒ	Ⓓ

2. I will help take good _____ of the kitten.

pail	pictures	care	sash
Ⓐ	Ⓑ	Ⓒ	Ⓓ

3. We each got a new _____ of shoes.

kind	pair	snap	said
Ⓐ	Ⓑ	Ⓒ	Ⓓ

4. I did not _____ to break anything in that store!

dare	want	crank	far
Ⓐ	Ⓑ	Ⓒ	Ⓓ

STOP

DECODING/PHONICS

b**oo**k   c**ou**ld

Sample

Will you _____ over there?

soon   stand   look   mole
Ⓐ   Ⓑ   Ⓒ   Ⓓ

---

5. We _____ always be kind to others.

cold   should   will   stick
Ⓐ   Ⓑ   Ⓒ   Ⓓ

6. Hang your coat on that _____.

night   noon   hook   rack
Ⓐ   Ⓑ   Ⓒ   Ⓓ

7. We will _____ hot dogs on the grill.

cook   shop   make   room
Ⓐ   Ⓑ   Ⓒ   Ⓓ

8. If you _____ help me, I might finish.

deer   would   can   found
Ⓐ   Ⓑ   Ⓒ   Ⓓ

STOP

Score_____   *Banner Days / Theme 3*

Harcourt • Reading and Language Skills Assessment

DECODING/PHONICS

<u>dau</u>ghter   c<u>law</u>

Sample

Dena is my _____.

shell   daughter   laugh   sister

Ⓐ   Ⓑ   Ⓒ   Ⓓ

---

9. Your _____ looks pretty and green.

lawn   shave   yard   sharp

Ⓐ   Ⓑ   Ⓒ   Ⓓ

10. He did not get a treat because he had been _____.

day   naughty   bad   nut

Ⓐ   Ⓑ   Ⓒ   Ⓓ

11. Can you _____ a picture of a lion?

sun   trace   sand   draw

Ⓐ   Ⓑ   Ⓒ   Ⓓ

12. The fox was _____ in the trap.

caught   change   tune   stuck

Ⓐ   Ⓑ   Ⓒ   Ⓓ

STOP

DECODING/PHONICS

y<u>ou</u>th   **thr<u>ough</u>**

Sample

I have a _____ for a free bag of popcorn.

need	crop	luck	coupon
Ⓐ	Ⓑ	Ⓒ	Ⓓ

---

13. We ate _____ for supper.

hut	soup	cheese	code
Ⓐ	Ⓑ	Ⓒ	Ⓓ

14. The doctor will take care of that _____ on your arm.

wound	club	cut	rush
Ⓐ	Ⓑ	Ⓒ	Ⓓ

15. We went _____ the door and into a big room.

stole	out	through	still
Ⓐ	Ⓑ	Ⓒ	Ⓓ

16. I want to play with _____ today.

trot	you	dunk	toys
Ⓐ	Ⓑ	Ⓒ	Ⓓ

STOP

Harcourt • Reading and Language Skills Assessment

DECODING/PHONICS

Sample

Our team won first prize because we were _____ in every game.

beating	unbeaten	overbeat	beats
Ⓐ	Ⓑ	Ⓒ	Ⓓ

17. My shoe came _____, so I had to tie it again.

overtied	tying	untied	tie
Ⓐ	Ⓑ	Ⓒ	Ⓓ

18. Do not _____ the cake, or it will taste dry.

cooks	overcook	cooking	uncook
Ⓐ	Ⓑ	Ⓒ	Ⓓ

19. The dirty water was _____ for drinking.

unfit	fits	fitting	overfit
Ⓐ	Ⓑ	Ⓒ	Ⓓ

20. Do not _____, or you won't have room for pie.

uneat	overeat	eats	eating
Ⓐ	Ⓑ	Ⓒ	Ⓓ

STOP

VOCABULARY: Homophones

Sample: Which sentence is wrong?

Ⓐ The <u>bear</u> growled.

Ⓑ She has <u>two</u> pets.

Ⓒ Mom put <u>flour</u> in the cake.

Ⓓ Would you like a ripe <u>pair</u> to eat?

---

21. Ⓐ Come over <u>here</u>, please.

Ⓑ We <u>eight</u> hot dogs.

Ⓒ What a pretty <u>flower</u>!

Ⓓ Is my answer <u>right</u>?

22. Ⓐ <u>Would</u> you help me?

Ⓑ We put water in a <u>pail</u>.

Ⓒ Put the box over <u>they're</u>.

Ⓓ The boat has a white <u>sail</u>.

23. Ⓐ Let's go <u>to</u> the store.

Ⓑ I read a fairy <u>tale</u>.

Ⓒ There is something in my <u>eye</u>.

Ⓓ The ship sailed on the <u>see</u>.

24. Ⓐ Do you <u>no</u> the answer?

Ⓑ I can <u>write</u> my name.

Ⓒ They forgot <u>their</u> tickets.

Ⓓ I have a new <u>pair</u> of shoes.

STOP

Score _____

COMPREHENSION: Locate Information

granddaughter		knelt

grand·daugh·ter [grand′dôt•ər] The daughter of a person's son or daughter: **The grandparents took care of their little** *granddaughter* **while her parents worked.**

grew [gro͞o] Got bigger: **The little tree** *grew* **to be very tall.** grow, grown, growing

hand·some [han′səm] Good-looking: **A tiger has a** *handsome* **striped coat.**

hard·ly [härd′lē] Almost not: **He could** *hardly* **lift the heavy box.**

homework [hōm′wûrk] Schoolwork done at home: **Our teacher gives us** *homework* **every night.**

knelt [nelt] Got down on one's knees: **He** *knelt* **down to pick up the pen he had dropped.** kneel, kneeling

knelt

Sample

What are the guide words on this page?

(A) granddaughter—knelt

(B) granddaughter—homework

(C) grew—handsome

(D) hardly—homework

GO ON ▶

COMPREHENSION: Locate Information (continued)

snug		tame

snug [snug] Warm and comfortable: **The children were *snug* in their warm beds that winter night.** *syn.* cozy

spar·kling [spär′kling] Shining in the light as a jewel does: **The dew on the grass was *sparkling* in the sunlight.** sparkle, sparkled *syn.* glittering

sprout [sprout] Begin to grow: **When the seeds *sprout*, tiny plants will push up through the ground.** sprouted, sprouting

sur·vive [sər·vīv′] To stay alive: **Desert plants and animals can *survive* without much water.** survived, surviving

tame [tām] To make something less wild: **You should not try to *tame* a wild animal by petting it.** tamed, taming

25. Here is part of a Glossary page. Which word means almost the same as *snug*?

Ⓐ cozy

Ⓑ glittering

Ⓒ useful

Ⓓ ruined

26. What is the meaning of *survive*?

Ⓐ to hold close

Ⓑ to begin to grow

Ⓒ to stay alive

Ⓓ to make something less wild

GO ON ▶

COMPREHENSION: Locate Information (continued)

Index *of* Titles

Page numbers in color tell where you can read about the author.

All Join In, 188	
Ancona, George, 174, 187	
Appelt, Kathi, 368, 389	
Blake, Quentin, 188	
Brigham, Tina, 220	
Carle, Eric, 16, 46	
Chevallier, Chiara, 340	
Days with Frog and Toad, 102	
deSpain, Pleasant, 286, 305	
Enormous Turnip, The, 154	
Fisher, Aileen, 306	
From Seed to Plant, 314	
"From Seed to Plant" Project, A, 332	
Fun Animal Facts: Chameleons, 48	
Get Up and Go!, 56	
Gibbons, Gail, 314, 331, 332	
Hedgehog Bakes a Cake, 228	
Hedgehog's Yellow Cake, 248	
Helping Out, 174	
Henry and Mudge Under the Yellow Moon, 84	
Hess, Debra, 126, 145	

462

27. Here is part of an Index of Titles and Authors. On which page would you find "Days with Frog and Toad"?

   Ⓐ page 16   Ⓑ page 102

   Ⓒ page 174   Ⓓ page 220

28. On which page would you find something written by Tina Brigham?

   Ⓐ page 46   Ⓑ page 174

   Ⓒ page 220   Ⓓ page 340

GO ON ▶

COMPREHENSION: Locate Information (continued)

CONTENTS

Johnny Appleseed 284
by Pleasant deSpain

The Seed 306
by Aileen Fisher

Phonics Skill Words with *ear* and *eer*

From Seed to Plant 312
by Gail Gibbons

A "From Seed to Plant" Project 332
by Gail Gibbons

Focus Skill Information from Diagrams

The Secret Life of Trees 338
by Chiara Chevallier

Leaf Zoo 360
from *Your Big Backyard*

29. Here is part of a Table of Contents page. Which author wrote "From Seed to Plant"?

- Ⓐ Pleasant deSpain
- Ⓑ Aileen Fisher
- Ⓒ Gail Gibbons
- Ⓓ Chiara Chevallier

30. Which of these did Aileen Fisher write?

- Ⓐ "Johnny Appleseed"
- Ⓑ "The Seed"
- Ⓒ "From Seed to Plant"
- Ⓓ "The Secret Life of Trees"

STOP

Harcourt • Reading and Language Skills Assessment

LANGUAGE

Sample

Yesterday we <u>give</u> the dog a bath.

(A) gives

(B) gave

(C) correct as is

---

31. My aunt greets me and <u>give</u> me a hug.

(A) gives

(B) gave

(C) correct as is

32. Now she <u>do</u> the shopping.

(A) did

(B) does

(C) correct as is

33. Yesterday I <u>see</u> a squirrel in a tree.

(A) sees

(B) saw

(C) correct as is

GO ON

Harcourt • Reading and Language Skills Assessment

LANGUAGE (continued)

34. Do you <u>see</u> that kite in the sky?

Ⓐ sees

Ⓑ saw

Ⓒ correct as is

35. Last week my parents <u>goes</u> out of town.

Ⓐ go

Ⓑ went

Ⓒ correct as is

36. Now our newspaper <u>come</u> each morning by 6:00 A.M.

Ⓐ comes

Ⓑ came

Ⓒ correct as is

37. You should <u>runs</u> for the bus before it leaves.

Ⓐ run

Ⓑ ran

Ⓒ correct as is

GO ON

Harcourt • Reading and Language Skills Assessment

LANGUAGE (continued)

38. Last week my brother <u>run</u> a mile every day.

(A) runs

(B) ran

(C) correct as is

39. Which word is the helping verb in this sentence?
The little chicks have chirped for hours.

(A) little

(B) chicks

(C) have

40. Which word is the helping verb in this sentence?
That man has trimmed the bushes.

(A) man

(B) has

(C) trimmed

STOP

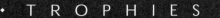
· T R O P H I E S ·

Travel Time / Theme 3
Reading and Language Skills Assessment

Harcourt

Orlando   Boston   Dallas   Chicago   San Diego

Part No. 9997-37722-2

ISBN 0-15-332183-0 (Package of 12)

2-2

TROPHIES

Reading and Language Skills Assessment Posttest

Banner Days / Theme 3

Name_____ Date_____

SKILL AREA	Criterion Score	Pupil Score	Pupil Strength
DECODING/PHONICS			
R-controlled Vowels			
/âr/*air, are*	3/4	_____	_____
Vowel Variants			
/o͞o/*oo, ou*	3/4	_____	_____
/ô/*aw, au(gh)*	3/4	_____	_____
Vowel Digraphs			
/o͞o/*ou, ou(gh)*	3/4	_____	_____
Prefixes			
over-, un-	3/4	_____	_____
VOCABULARY			
Homophones	3/4	_____	_____
COMPREHENSION			
Locate Information: Book Parts	4/6	_____	_____
LANGUAGE	7/10	_____	_____
See, Give, Saw, Gave			
Come, Run, Came, Ran			
Go, Do, Went, Did			
Helping Verbs			
TOTAL SCORE	29/40	_____	_____

Were accommodations made in administering this test?   ☐ Yes   ☐ No

Type of accommodations: _____

_____

Printed in the United States of America

ISBN 0-15-332183-0

6 7 8 9 10   170   10 09 08 07 06 05 04

DECODING/PHONICS

chair   **bare**

Sample

Will you _____ your toys?

mad   star   share   bring
Ⓐ   Ⓑ   Ⓒ   Ⓓ

---

1. The cake pan has a _____ shape.

par   square   cold   circle
Ⓐ   Ⓑ   Ⓒ   Ⓓ

2. My grandma has pretty white_____.

yell   rain   hair   teeth
Ⓐ   Ⓑ   Ⓒ   Ⓓ

3. We will meet Uncle Lee at the_____.

jar   airport   save   park
Ⓐ   Ⓑ   Ⓒ   Ⓓ

4. Be _____ not to trip on that step.

careful   sure   crank   yard
Ⓐ   Ⓑ   Ⓒ   Ⓓ

STOP

DECODING/PHONICS

b<u>oo</u>k   **c<u>ou</u>ld**

Sample

Will you _____ over there?

soon   stand   look   mole
Ⓐ   Ⓑ   Ⓒ   Ⓓ

---

5. I stepped on something sharp and hurt my _____.

sheet   zoo   foot   heel
Ⓐ   Ⓑ   Ⓒ   Ⓓ

6. You _____ be careful on the slick ice.

should   rake   will   found
Ⓐ   Ⓑ   Ⓒ   Ⓓ

7. I love to read a good _____.

dish   book   roof   story
Ⓐ   Ⓑ   Ⓒ   Ⓓ

8. Mom said that I _____ go on the trip.

ship   could   might   mouth
Ⓐ   Ⓑ   Ⓒ   Ⓓ

STOP

Harcourt • Reading and Language Skills Assessment

DECODING/PHONICS

da<u>ugh</u>ter   **cl<u>aw</u>**

Sample

Dena is my _____ .

shell	daughter	laugh	sister
Ⓐ	Ⓑ	Ⓒ	Ⓓ

---

9. I always _____ when I get sleepy.

crane	sub	yawn	rest
Ⓐ	Ⓑ	Ⓒ	Ⓓ

10. My teacher _____ me how to write my name.

taught	club	showed	catch
Ⓐ	Ⓑ	Ⓒ	Ⓓ

11. Look at that _____ flying in the sky.

yolk	lake	bird	hawk
Ⓐ	Ⓑ	Ⓒ	Ⓓ

12. At puppy school, our pup learns not to be_____ .

throw	thank	naughty	loud
Ⓐ	Ⓑ	Ⓒ	Ⓓ

STOP

DECODING/PHONICS

<u>y</u>**outh**   **thr**<u>ough</u>

Sample

I have a _____ for a free bag of popcorn.

need   crop   luck   coupon
Ⓐ   Ⓑ   Ⓒ   Ⓓ

---

13. We searched _____ the house for my lost book.

throughout   seat   mole   all
Ⓐ   Ⓑ   Ⓒ   Ⓓ

14. We have a new friend in our _____.

group   club   rope   puck
Ⓐ   Ⓑ   Ⓒ   Ⓓ

15. Does this bike belong to _____?

crush   him   size   you
Ⓐ   Ⓑ   Ⓒ   Ⓓ

16. I like to eat chicken _____.

dune   soup   sandwiches   jog
Ⓐ   Ⓑ   Ⓒ   Ⓓ

STOP

Harcourt • Reading and Language Skills Assessment

DECODING/PHONICS

Sample

Our team won first prize because we were _____ in every game.

beating	unbeaten	overbeat	beats
Ⓐ	Ⓑ	Ⓒ	Ⓓ

17. The tub will _____ if I forget and leave the water running.

flowed	flows	overflow	unflow
Ⓐ	Ⓑ	Ⓒ	Ⓓ

18. If your key will _____ the door, we can go inside.

locked	unlock	overlock	locks
Ⓐ	Ⓑ	Ⓒ	Ⓓ

19. Do not _____, or you will get tired.

overwork	worked	unwork	works
Ⓐ	Ⓑ	Ⓒ	Ⓓ

20. Why don't you _____ the dog so he can run free for a while?

leashed	overleash	leashing	unleash
Ⓐ	Ⓑ	Ⓒ	Ⓓ

STOP

VOCABULARY: Homophones

Sample: Which sentence is wrong?
- Ⓐ The <u>bear</u> growled.
- Ⓑ She has <u>two</u> pets.
- Ⓒ Mom put <u>flour</u> in the cake.
- Ⓓ Would you like a ripe <u>pair</u> to eat?

21.
- Ⓐ Can you <u>hear</u> me?
- Ⓑ I will <u>write</u> to you.
- Ⓒ Read me a fairy <u>tail</u>.
- Ⓓ We <u>ate</u> pizza last night.

22.
- Ⓐ <u>Wood</u> you play with me?
- Ⓑ I want to go, <u>too</u>.
- Ⓒ <u>Here</u> are your books.
- Ⓓ The butter is <u>pale</u> yellow.

23.
- Ⓐ Dad will chop the <u>wood</u>.
- Ⓑ Sit over <u>hear</u> by me.
- Ⓒ The toys are on <u>sale</u>.
- Ⓓ Do you <u>see</u> that star?

24.
- Ⓐ The spider has <u>eight</u> legs.
- Ⓑ We saw a <u>bear</u> at the zoo.
- Ⓒ I have <u>no</u> chores to do.
- Ⓓ Do I turn left or <u>write</u>?

STOP

Score _____   *Banner Days / Theme 3*

COMPREHENSION: Locate Information

granddaughter		knelt

grand·daugh·ter [grand′dôt•ər] The daughter of a person's son or
daughter: **The grandparents took care of their little**
***granddaughter* while her parents worked.**

grew [grōō] Got bigger: **The little tree *grew* to be very tall.** grow,
grown, growing

hand·some [han′səm] Good-looking: **A tiger has a *handsome***
striped coat.

hard·ly [härd′lē] Almost not: **He could *hardly* lift the heavy box.**

homework [hōm′wûrk] Schoolwork done at home: **Our teacher**
gives us *homework* every night.

knelt

knelt [nelt] Got down on one's knees: **He *knelt* down to pick up the**
pen he had dropped. kneel, kneeling

Sample

What are the guide words on this page?

Ⓐ granddaughter—knelt

Ⓑ granddaughter—homework

Ⓒ grew—handsome

Ⓓ hardly—homework

GO ON

COMPREHENSION: Locate Information (continued)

snug   tame

> **snug** [snug] Warm and comfortable: **The children were *snug* in their warm beds that winter night.** *syn.* cozy
>
> **spar·kling** [spär′kling] Shining in the light as a jewel does: **The dew on the grass was *sparkling* in the sunlight.** sparkle, sparkled *syn.* glittering
>
> **sprout** [sprout] Begin to grow: **When the seeds *sprout*, tiny plants will push up through the ground.** sprouted, sprouting
>
> **sur·vive** [sər·vīv′] To stay alive: **Desert plants and animals can *survive* without much water.** survived, surviving
>
>
>
> **tame** [tām] To make something less wild: **You should not try to *tame* a wild animal by petting it.** tamed, taming

25. Here is part of a Glossary page. Which word means almost the same as *sparkling*?

Ⓐ cozy

Ⓑ glittering

Ⓒ useful

Ⓓ ruined

26. What is the meaning of *sprout*?

Ⓐ to hold close

Ⓑ to begin to grow

Ⓒ to stay alive

Ⓓ to make something less wild

GO ON ▶

COMPREHENSION: Locate Information (continued)

Index *of* Titles

Page numbers in color tell where you can read about the author.

All Join In, 188
Ancona, George, 174, 187
Appelt, Kathi, 368, 389
Blake, Quentin, 188
Brigham, Tina, 220
Carle, Eric, 16, 46
Chevallier, Chiara, 340
Days with Frog and Toad, 102
deSpain, Pleasant, 286, 305
Enormous Turnip, The, 154
Fisher, Aileen, 306
From Seed to Plant, 314
"From Seed to Plant" Project, A, 332
Fun Animal Facts: Chameleons, 48
Get Up and Go!, 56
Gibbons, Gail, 314, 331, 332
Hedgehog Bakes a Cake, 228
Hedgehog's Yellow Cake, 248
Helping Out, 174
Henry and Mudge Under the Yellow Moon, 84
Hess, Debra, 126, 145

462

27. Here is part of an Index of Titles and Authors. On which page would you find "The Enormous Turnip"?

Ⓐ page 16   Ⓑ page 102

Ⓒ page 154   Ⓓ page 220

28. On which page would you find something written by Quentin Blake?

Ⓐ page 188   Ⓑ page 174

Ⓒ page 340   Ⓓ page 389

GO ON

COMPREHENSION: Locate Information (continued)

CONTENTS

> Phonics Skill Words with *ear* and *eer*

> Focus Skill Information from Diagrams

29. Here is part of a Table of Contents page. Which author wrote "The Secret Life of Trees"?

Ⓐ Pleasant deSpain

Ⓑ Aileen Fisher

Ⓒ Gail Gibbons

Ⓓ Chiara Chevallier

30. Which of these did Pleasant deSpain write?

Ⓐ "Johnny Appleseed"

Ⓑ "The Seed"

Ⓒ "From Seed to Plant"

Ⓓ "The Secret Life of Trees"

STOP

Harcourt • Reading and Language Skills Assessment

LANGUAGE

Sample

Yesterday we <u>give</u> the dog a bath.

Ⓐ gives

Ⓑ gave

Ⓒ correct as is

31. Now he <u>do</u> his homework.

Ⓐ did

Ⓑ does

Ⓒ correct as is

32. Dad hugs me and <u>gives</u> me a surprise.

Ⓐ give

Ⓑ gave

Ⓒ correct as is

33. Yesterday I <u>sees</u> some ducks on the lake.

Ⓐ see

Ⓑ saw

Ⓒ correct as is

GO ON

LANGUAGE (continued)

34. Do you <u>sees</u> that shooting star?

    Ⓐ see

    Ⓑ saw

    Ⓒ correct as is

35. Last week my sister <u>go</u> to a play.

    Ⓐ goes

    Ⓑ went

    Ⓒ correct as is

36. Our neighbor <u>come</u> to our house for lunch yesterday.

    Ⓐ came

    Ⓑ comes

    Ⓒ correct as is

37. You should <u>ran</u> in the school relay race.

    Ⓐ run

    Ⓑ runs

    Ⓒ correct as is

GO ON

LANGUAGE (continued)

38. Yesterday I <u>run</u> to catch the bus.

Ⓐ runs

Ⓑ ran

Ⓒ correct as is

39. Which word is the helping verb in this sentence?

My friend has eaten all his carrots.

Ⓐ My

Ⓑ friend

Ⓒ has

40. Which word is the helping verb in this sentence?

All the children have won prizes.

Ⓐ All

Ⓑ have

Ⓒ won

STOP

Harcourt • Reading and Language Skills Assessment

· T R O P H I E S ·

Travel Time / Theme 3
Reading and Language Skills Assessment

Harcourt

Orlando   Boston   Dallas   Chicago   San Diego

Part No. 9997-37719-2

ISBN 0-15-332183-0 (Package of 12)

2-2

· TROPHIES ·

End-of-Year Reading and Language Skills Assessment

Grade 2 / Themes 1–6

Name_____ Date_____

SKILL AREA	Criterion Score	Pupil Score	Comments
DECODING/PHONICS	16/22	_____	_____
VOCABULARY	4/6	_____	_____
COMPREHENSION	6/8	_____	_____
LITERARY RESPONSE AND ANALYSIS	3/4	_____	_____
LANGUAGE	7/10	_____	_____
TOTAL SCORE	**36/50**	_____	_____

Were accommodations made in administering this test? ❏ Yes ❏ No

Type of accommodations: _____

_____

DECODING/PHONICS

<u>out</u>   **<u>cow</u>**

Sample

Look at that _____ in the sky.

bird   joke   cloud   four
Ⓐ   Ⓑ   Ⓒ   Ⓓ

---

1. We just moved to a new _____.

sky   house   pour   city
Ⓐ   Ⓑ   Ⓒ   Ⓓ

2. I do not know _____ to do this.

when   tub   how   crow
Ⓐ   Ⓑ   Ⓒ   Ⓓ

STOP

DECODING/PHONICS

<u>co</u>in   <u>oy</u>ster

Sample

May I play with your _____ truck?

try   new   toy   grow
Ⓐ   Ⓑ   Ⓒ   Ⓓ

---

3. Just _____ to the puppy you want.

point   bright   call   chop
Ⓐ   Ⓑ   Ⓒ   Ⓓ

4. Will you give me a _____ to throw in the wishing well?

song   damp   coin   penny
Ⓐ   Ⓑ   Ⓒ   Ⓓ

STOP

DECODING/PHONICS

s<u>oo</u>n   cl<u>ue</u>   br<u>ui</u>se   gr<u>ew</u>   y<u>ou</u>   thr<u>ough</u>

Sample

The color I like best is _____.

green   drum   tale   blue
Ⓐ   Ⓑ   Ⓒ   Ⓓ

---

5. A bird just _____ in the window.

flew   book   clay   came
Ⓐ   Ⓑ   Ⓒ   Ⓓ

6. The teacher told us to stand in a _____.

robin   group   line   found
Ⓐ   Ⓑ   Ⓒ   Ⓓ

STOP

DECODING/PHONICS

Sample

They say that cats have nine _____.

life	lifes	lives	lifs
Ⓐ	Ⓑ	Ⓒ	Ⓓ

---

7. That tree has lost all its _____.

leafes	leaves	leaf	leafies
Ⓐ	Ⓑ	Ⓒ	Ⓓ

8. Our room at school has many _____ for books.

shelfs	shelf	shelves	shelfies
Ⓐ	Ⓑ	Ⓒ	Ⓓ

STOP

DECODING/PHONICS

Sample

I am very _____ for your help.

thank   thanking   thankful   thankless
Ⓐ   Ⓑ   Ⓒ   Ⓓ

---

9. Do not be _____, or you will drop those eggs.

care   carefully   careless   cared
Ⓐ   Ⓑ   Ⓒ   Ⓓ

10. I hope the tools I gave you will be _____ to you.

uses   useful   using   useless
Ⓐ   Ⓑ   Ⓒ   Ⓓ

STOP

DECODING/PHONICS

Sample

I <u>do not</u> have the key.

didn't	don't	can't	won't
Ⓐ	Ⓑ	Ⓒ	Ⓓ

11. <u>They will</u> arrive soon.

We'll	You'll	He'll	They'll
Ⓐ	Ⓑ	Ⓒ	Ⓓ

12. Do you think <u>it is</u> going to rain?

that's	it's	he's	who's
Ⓐ	Ⓑ	Ⓒ	Ⓓ

STOP

Harcourt • Reading and Language Skills Assessment

DECODING/PHONICS

Sample

The little mole has a home deep_____.

grounded   underground   reground   grounding
Ⓐ   Ⓑ   Ⓒ   Ⓓ

---

13. I will _____ your things to you tomorrow.

turning   return   turned   misturn
Ⓐ   Ⓑ   Ⓒ   Ⓓ

14. Be careful not to _____ the tickets.

miscount   counted   uncount   counting
Ⓐ   Ⓑ   Ⓒ   Ⓓ

STOP

DECODING/PHONICS

Sample

I am the _____ of the three children in our family.

old	older	oldest	olds
Ⓐ	Ⓑ	Ⓒ	Ⓓ

15. That oak tree is _____ than this pine tree.

tall	taller	tallest	talls
Ⓐ	Ⓑ	Ⓒ	Ⓓ

16. This is the _____ peach of all.

sweet	sweeter	sweetest	sweets
Ⓐ	Ⓑ	Ⓒ	Ⓓ

STOP

Harcourt • Reading and Language Skills Assessment

DECODING/PHONICS

ch**ai**r   **bare**

Sample

Will you _____ your toys?

mad	star	share	bring
Ⓐ	Ⓑ	Ⓒ	Ⓓ

17. Be careful not to _____ the little pup away.

scare	bar	frighten	try
Ⓐ	Ⓑ	Ⓒ	Ⓓ

18. Will you _____ the flat tire on my bike?

soft	glide	fix	repair
Ⓐ	Ⓑ	Ⓒ	Ⓓ

STOP

DECODING/PHONICS

---

b**oo**k   c**oul**d

Sample

Will you _____ over there?

soon   stand   look   mole
Ⓐ   Ⓑ   Ⓒ   Ⓓ

---

19. Fish were swimming in the little _____.

hill   broom   brook   stream
Ⓐ   Ⓑ   Ⓒ   Ⓓ

20. You _____ always have good manners.

bank   should   must   ground
Ⓐ   Ⓑ   Ⓒ   Ⓓ

STOP

Harcourt • Reading and Language Skills Assessment

DECODING/PHONICS

da<u>ugh</u>ter **cl<u>aw</u>**

Sample

Dena is my _____.

shell   daughter   laugh   sister
Ⓐ   Ⓑ   Ⓒ   Ⓓ

21. That little pup has hurt its _____.

paw   cave   leg   truck
Ⓐ   Ⓑ   Ⓒ   Ⓓ

22. Have you _____ any fish yet?

prune   seen   dash   caught
Ⓐ   Ⓑ   Ⓒ   Ⓓ

STOP

Harcourt • Reading and Language Skills Assessment

VOCABULARY

Sample

The opposite of <u>back</u> is _____.

Ⓐ sun

Ⓑ dark

Ⓒ front

Ⓓ girl

---

23. The opposite of <u>dangerous</u> is _____.

Ⓐ light

Ⓑ safe

Ⓒ dirty

Ⓓ friendly

24. The opposite of <u>completely</u> is _____.

Ⓐ partly

Ⓑ differently

Ⓒ hopefully

Ⓓ thankfully

GO ON

End-of-Year Skills

VOCABULARY (continued)

25. Read this sentence.

I need one foot of paper to cover the package.

What does the word *foot* mean in this sentence?

(A) 12 inches in length

(B) bottom of a ladder

(C) end part of a leg

(D) end of the bed

26. Read this sentence.

Watch out for that big dip in the road.

In which sentence does the word dip mean the same thing as in the sentence above?

(A) I will dip the egg into the dye.

(B) We are eating cheese dip and chips.

(C) Let's go for a dip in the swimming pool.

(D) We slowed down for the dip in the highway.

GO ON

VOCABULARY (continued)

27. Which sentence is wrong?

Ⓐ I can <u>see</u> far away.

Ⓑ I broke my new <u>pear</u> of glasses.

Ⓒ She went to get a <u>pail</u> of water.

Ⓓ Please stand over <u>there</u>.

28. Which sentence is wrong?

Ⓐ I <u>would</u> be happy to see you again.

Ⓑ Sift the <u>flour</u> before you add it to the batter.

Ⓒ Are you going <u>too</u> the pet shop?

Ⓓ <u>They're</u> my best pictures.

STOP

Score_____

Harcourt • Reading and Language Skills Assessment

COMPREHENSION

A small dog followed Jan home from school. He was very thin, and he looked hungry. "May we keep him?" Jan asked her mother.

"I don't think so," Mother said. "He might belong to someone. We need to find his owner."

"How can we do that?" Jan asked.

"Your father and I will work on that. While we do, you may take care of him and play with him, but don't get your hopes up about keeping him."

Sample

Mother says they must look for the dog's owner because she _____.

Ⓐ does not care if the dog is hungry

Ⓑ thinks the dog might belong to someone

Ⓒ likes cats more than she likes dogs

Ⓓ wants Jan to get a different kind of dog

GO ON

COMPREHENSION (continued)

Frogs lay eggs in different places. Some frogs lay their eggs deep in the water where they will not freeze. Other frogs lay their eggs near the top of the water. Some frogs lay their eggs in wet leaves or moss.

Frog eggs hatch about four to fifteen days after they are laid. A little *tadpole* hatches from an egg. Different kinds of frogs lay different colors of eggs and have different kinds of tadpoles.

Frogs may lay hundreds or thousands of eggs at one time. Not all the frogs grow up, though, because many frog eggs get eaten by fish, by insects, and by other water animals.

29. What is the main idea of the first paragraph?
  (A) Some frogs lay their eggs in wet leaves.
  (B) Frogs lay eggs in different places.
  (C) Some frogs lay their eggs in deep water.
  (D) Some frogs lay their eggs near the top of the water.

30. Why do some frogs lay their eggs deep in the water?
  (A) to keep the eggs away from insects
  (B) so that the eggs will not freeze
  (C) so that the eggs will not dry out
  (D) to keep water animals from seeing the eggs

GO ON

Harcourt • Reading and Language Skills Assessment

COMPREHENSION (continued)

31. How many eggs might a frog lay at one time?

(A) 1

(B) 4

(C) 15

(D) 100 or more

32. Why don't all frog eggs become grown-up frogs?

(A) Most of the eggs will never hatch.

(B) Some tadpoles will not learn to swim.

(C) Fish, insects, or water animals will eat many of the eggs.

(D) Some colors of eggs are not as strong as other colors.

GO ON

Harcourt • Reading and Language Skills Assessment

COMPREHENSION (continued)

Meg and Ron went to a farm. First, they helped Farmer Fred feed the chickens. Next, they helped gather eggs that the hens had laid. After that, the children watched Farmer Fred milk the cows.

33. Which is the best summary of this story?

Ⓐ First, Meg and Ron helped Farmer Fred feed the chickens.

Ⓑ Meg and Ron went to a farm, helped feed chickens and gather eggs, and watched Farmer Fred milk the cows.

Ⓒ Next, Meg and Ron helped gather eggs that the hens had laid.

Ⓓ After gathering eggs, Meg and Ron watched Farmer Fred milk the cows.

GO ON

Harcourt • Reading and Language Skills Assessment

COMPREHENSION (continued)

34. The guide words *simple* and *sprout* are on a glossary page. Which other word could be found on that page?

Ⓐ beneath

Ⓑ enormous

Ⓒ groups

Ⓓ sniffing

35. What is the **best** place to look to find out the meaning of *dusky*?

Ⓐ the index

Ⓑ the glossary

Ⓒ the table of contents

Ⓓ chapter headings

36. What is the **best** place to look to find out the chapter headings in *Harry Potter and the Chamber of Secrets?*

Ⓐ the index

Ⓑ the glossary

Ⓒ the table of contents

Ⓓ the book cover

STOP

LITERARY RESPONSE AND ANALYSIS

Henry and Maria went to the zoo one morning. First, they went to see the lions. One of the lions roared loudly as it moved around in its cage. The children hurried away from the lion's cage and went to see the monkeys.

The monkeys were fun to watch. They jumped around and made a lot of noise. Maria and Henry threw them some nuts to eat.

Then, the children saw a man selling balloons. The balloons were in all different colors, and they looked like zoo animals! Maria got a yellow balloon that looked like a tiger. She couldn't wait to show it to Aunt Teresa.

Sample

Who is this story mostly about?

Ⓐ Henry and Maria

Ⓑ Aunt Teresa

Ⓒ the balloon man

Ⓓ a tiger

37. Where does this story take place?

Ⓐ at a balloon store

Ⓑ at the zoo

Ⓒ on a farm

Ⓓ in a pet store

GO ON

End-of-Year Skills

Harcourt • Reading and Language Skills Assessment

LITERARY RESPONSE AND ANALYSIS (continued)

38. When does the story take place?

Ⓐ at bed time

Ⓑ during lunch

Ⓒ in the morning

Ⓓ in the evening

39. What do Henry and Maria see **first**?

Ⓐ a man selling balloons

Ⓑ tigers

Ⓒ monkeys

Ⓓ lions

40. What did Maria and Henry do when the lion roared?

Ⓐ watched the lion eat

Ⓑ called for help

Ⓒ ran to the zoo keeper

Ⓓ went to see the monkeys

STOP

Harcourt • Reading and Language Skills Assessment

LANGUAGE

Sample

Which word is a pronoun in this sentence?
She likes ice cream.

(A) She

(B) likes

(C) ice cream

---

41. Which is the best pronoun for the underlined words?

The eggs are hatching now.

(A) It

(B) He

(C) They

42. Which answer tells about the underlined words?

The ship sails across the glassy sea.

(A) naming part

(B) telling part

(C) complete sentence

43. Which word is a noun in this sentence?

Four geese are swimming.

(A) Four

(B) geese

(C) are

GO ON

Harcourt • Reading and Language Skills Assessment

LANGUAGE (continued)

44. Which word is a describing word in this sentence?

We looked at the bright star in the sky.

Ⓐ We

Ⓑ looked

Ⓒ bright

45. Which describing word tells how many in this sentence?

There are many chickens in the coop.

Ⓐ are

Ⓑ many

Ⓒ chickens

46. Which word best completes this sentence?

She has a _____ voice than he does.

Ⓐ softer

Ⓑ softest

Ⓒ soft

47. Which word is the verb in this sentence?

The clouds drift in the sky.

Ⓐ clouds

Ⓑ drift

Ⓒ sky

GO ON

Harcourt • Reading and Language Skills Assessment

LANGUAGE (continued)

48. Which verb tells about now to complete this sentence?

Now I <u>does</u> all the work.

Ⓐ do

Ⓑ did

Ⓒ correct as is

49. Which verb tells about the past to complete this sentence?

Last week I _____ a sore throat.

Ⓐ has

Ⓑ have

Ⓒ had

50. Which sentence begins and ends correctly?

Ⓐ please close the door?

Ⓑ How handsome you look!

Ⓒ May I go with you.

STOP

Harcourt • Reading and Language Skills Assessment

· T R O P H I E S ·

Just for You/Banner Days

End-of-Year Reading and Language Skills Assessment

Harcourt

Orlando   Boston   Dallas   Chicago   San Diego

Part No. 9997-37723-0

ISBN 0-15-332183-0 (Package of 12)

2-2